Poor transitions

Social exclusion and young adults

Colin Webster, Donald Simpson, Robert MacDonald, Andrea Abbas, Mark Cieslik,
Tracy Shildrick and Mark Simpson

First published in Great Britain in December 2004 by

The Policy Press
Fourth Floor, Beacon House
Queen's Road
Bristol BS8 1QU
UK

Tel no +44 (0)117 331 4054
Fax no +44 (0)117 331 4093
E-mail tpp-info@bristol.ac.uk
www.policypress.org.uk

© University of Teesside 2004

Published for the Joseph Rowntree Foundation by The Policy Press

ISBN 1 86134 650 6

British Library Cataloguing in Publication Data
A catalogue record for this report is available from the British Library.

Library of Congress Cataloging-in-Publication Data
A catalog record for this report has been requested.

Colin Webster is Senior Lecturer in Criminology, **Donald Simpson** is a Researcher, **Robert MacDonald** is Professor of Sociology, **Andrea Abbas** is Senior Lecturer in Sociology, **Mark Cieslik** is Senior Lecturer in Sociology, **Tracy Shildrick** is Senior Lecturer in Sociology and **Mark Simpson** is Principal Lecturer in Criminology. All work in the School of Social Sciences and Law, University of Teesside.

The **Joseph Rowntree Foundation** has supported this project as part of its programme of research and innovative development projects, which it hopes will be of value to policy makers, practitioners and service users. The facts presented and views expressed in this report are, however, those of the authors and not necessarily those of the Foundation.

Cover design by Qube Design Associates, Bristol
Printed in Great Britain by Hobbs the Printers Ltd, Southampton

Contents

Acknowledgements

The authors wish to thank all the young adults participating in this research. Appreciation is also extended to Fiona, Darren and Maria for their help in producing interview transcripts. We also thank the Joseph Rowntree Foundation Advisory Group: Ruth Garratt, Carl Ditchburn, John Lambert, Tony Jones, Jane Marsh, and especially Bob Coles and Charlie Lloyd for their constructive and critical support.

Executive summary

This study set out to explore what had become of young people living in the poorest neighbourhoods of the poorest town in Britain, several years after we first contacted them. As they moved into young adulthood, had their longer-term experiences of disadvantage changed or stayed the same? While individuals reported feeling considerable *subjective* change in their lives, because of key turning points and critical moments (especially in respect of family and housing, and among offenders and dependent drug users), their *objective* circumstances had remained constant and their experiences of poverty persisted.

Despite continued commitment to finding and getting better work, most were still experiencing poor, low-waged, intermittent work at the bottom of the labour market. After obtaining poor school qualifications, further poor quality training and education had not improved their employment prospects. This lack of progression had ramifications in other aspects of their lives, resulting in social exclusion.

Among parents, and young mothers in particular, childcare responsibilities and the precariousness of childcare arrangements continued to restrict paid employment. Most chose to stay at home and delay employment to care for young children, in the context of lack of opportunities for decent, rewarding employment. The availability of childcare opportunities was more important than education, training and employment opportunities, but the former was a necessary condition for longer-term opportunities to be realised.

Most of those who had offended and/or were dependent drug users had, in the main, stopped offending and using heroin. This choice was facilitated through relinquishing earlier social networks, replaced by the support of family members and partners who discouraged offending and drug use. For some, employment or forming families of their own had further discouraged offending and drug use, and many were availing themselves of drug treatment services. Excluded from housing, employment and other choices because of their offending and drug-using histories, these supports offered first steps in a long, arduous struggle back to 'normal life'.

Most young adults had left their parental home and were living independently, although not always by choice. This had been helped by the plentiful supply of social housing. Those who remained in the parental home did so as a way of displacing and delaying the financial costs of independent living. Living with parents disguised – and eased – personal poverty. The quality and stability of relationships with families of origin were also an important influence on leaving or staying. A few had left the area, usually through forming new partnerships. There were emotional costs to leaving because of the physical separation from family and friends.

Earlier, restricted leisure patterns had continued and had become more home-based. Poverty, the heavy demands of childcare and domestic work and, for some of those in employment, the unsociable and long hours of the jobs they did, constrained leisure choices. Few had established ties into networks beyond their close personal associations. Their social networks had become smaller in scope, more focused on immediate family and friends and even more embedded in their immediate neighbourhoods. This further restricted wider support and longer-term education, training and employment opportunities.

Many had experienced bereavement through the death of people close to them. Although individuals responded to bereavement, ill-health and other serious life events in unpredictable ways, the social and personal consequences were often long term. Given the multiple hardships and instances of loss suffered, it is unsurprising that many reported experiences of depression.

A few individuals had more successful education, training and employment outcomes. The combination of a variety of positive experiences and circumstances created these more successful outcomes, the most important of which was having a good employer who encouraged and supported good quality education and training. For most however these positive experiences and circumstances were absent, or insufficient to be able to overcome the numerous, interconnected barriers and hurdles faced over time.

Despite numerous welfare and training initiatives in the study area over many years, the impoverished situations of most of our interviewees remained largely unchanged. Although programmes such as Child and Working Tax Credits, New Deal for Young People (NDYP) and Sure Start did improve some individuals' situations in ways that would otherwise not have occurred, they did not change the overall economically marginal position of those to whom we spoke. Indeed such initiatives, insofar as they rely on 'getting people into work' by making them 'more employable', in effect channel to, and then trap people in, poor quality and precarious work, thus encouraging rather than challenging the continuation of poor work. This study concludes that a fairer and more effective approach to facilitating successful moves into young adulthood in poor areas needs to address income redistribution through the tax and benefit system, and to ensure the creation of secure, decent jobs locally.

Introduction

This is a study of the longer-term transitions of young adults in neighbourhoods beset by the problems of social exclusion in extreme form. The research involved tracking participants from two earlier studies of socially disadvantaged 15- to 25-year-olds undertaken in north east England.

The first of these earlier studies, funded by the Joseph Rowntree Foundation (JRF) and published as *Snakes and Ladders* (Johnston et al, 2000), explored the range of 'mainstream' and 'alternative' careers that young people evolved in one small locale experiencing severe socioeconomic deprivation. A prime concern was to understand how young people, all from the Willowdene area of Kelby (all participants' names and place names are pseudonyms) and sharing similar social class locations, developed quite different youth transitions and outcomes. The second study, supported by the Economic and Social Research Council (ESRC), aimed to test the value of underclass theories and the concept of social exclusion in explaining youth transitions (MacDonald and Marsh, 2001, 2002a, 2002b, 2005). It was undertaken just a few miles from Willowdene in the five wards of East Kelby, a place labelled as one in which the 'new rabble underclass' might be found (Murray, 1994). These previous studies examined six important 'careers' that make up youth transitions:

- school-to-work career
- family career
- housing career
- leisure career
- drug-using career
- criminal career.

The previous studies found young people's transitions to be complex, non-linear, often disorderly and sometimes unpredictable. Many in the two samples were still experiencing complicated transitions in which they struggled to reach the normal goals associated with adulthood (for instance, many had been unable to find lasting, rewarding employment). Both projects, however, interviewed young men and women for whom extended school-to-work careers – and the getting of jobs – were, at that time, of secondary importance. Here two sub-groups are of particular interest to social scientific and policy analysis: young mothers and young men with sustained criminal and dependent drug-using careers.

'Miserable measures': a profile of deprived neighbourhoods

Together the earlier projects interviewed young people living in six wards of Kelby – a town in Teesside – north east England. Recent monitoring reveals that "across a range of indicators, problems of poverty and social exclusion are generally more prevalent in the north east than in other areas of the country" (New Policy Institute, 2003). The severe socioeconomic problems experienced in Kelby at the time of first interview continued and all but three people (from our sample of 34 participating in the current research) still lived in these wards. 'Joblessness rates' – that is, those people who are of working age (16-years-old to retirement) and not in paid employment – are an important measure of social disadvantage because of the high significance currently attached to paid employment as a means of escaping social exclusion. Table 1 shows how unfavourably our research sites compare with the town of Kelby as a whole, Tees Valley and the national situation.

Table 1: Joblessness: people of working age not in employment (October 2003)

	Male		Female		Total	
	Number	Rate (%)	Number	Rate (%)	Number	Rate (%)
Riverside	626	39.9	582	41.8	1,208	40.8
Willowdean	687	45.7	752	49.7	1,439	47.7
Brookville	782	41.3	936	46.5	1,719	44.0
Primrose Vale	613	41.0	871	51.9	1,484	46.8
Meadowfields	683	41.5	945	50.8	1,627	46.5
Orchard Bank	822	48.7	1,030	57.4	1,852	53.2
Kelby	14,100	34.3	16,450	40.8	30,600	37.5
Tees Valley	56,000	28.7	67,400	35.7	124,000	32.1
Great Britain	[a]	22.2	[a]	31.0	[a]	26.4

Note: [a] Data not available.

Source: ONS/Tees Valley Joint Strategy Unit

The Index of Multiple Deprivation (DETR, 2000) provides a broader estimation of the numerous problems of socially excluded places, and gives an overall rank for all districts and smaller wards in England. Kelby is the most multiply deprived district having the highest concentration of the most deprived wards in the country. In May 2003 there were 8,414 electoral wards in England. The Index showed that all six of the wards we studied were in the top 5% most deprived nationally and two of them (Orchard Bank and Primrose Vale) were in the worst five of the 8,414 in England (Reilly and Eynon, 2003).

Social exclusion and extended youth transitions

The primary focus of this research was on 'social exclusion' and 'extended youth transitions'. These two terms are now widely used – sometimes together – in policy, practice and academic debates.

Youth is a phase in the life-course between childhood and adulthood. Coles (2000) sees youth transitions as having three main dimensions: the move from full-time education into the labour market (the school-to-work career); the attainment of (relative) independence from family of origin (the family career); and the move away from the parental home (the housing career). Our own previous studies in Kelby suggested that, in some contexts, criminal careers, drug-using careers and leisure careers can also become important in shaping the overall nature of youth transitions (and these terms are

explained later in the report). These six aspects of transition became the foci of our interviews with young adults.

In recent decades, the effects of globalisation and de-industrialisation have resulted in youth transitions becoming extended. Alternatives to the traditional, quick movement from school to work made by working-class young people have evolved in which longer spells of post-16 training and further education play a greater part. Summarising much recent youth research, Jones (2002) stresses the hardening up of 'the youth divide' and the social polarisation of young people's experiences and life-chances. Those who make the speediest transitions into a youth labour market that has virtually 'collapsed', to parenthood and to independent living face far greater risks of the negative outcomes associated with social exclusion (Catan, 2003; Furlong and Cartmel, 1997). Recent longitudinal, survey research (Furlong et al, 2003) has attempted to demonstrate 'patterns of vulnerability and processes of social inclusion', particularly in respect of school-to-work careers. There remains a need, however, for studies that can help develop our understanding regarding "the nature of the links between different facets of disadvantage such as teenage pregnancy, drug use and continuing social exclusion" (Jones, 2002). Within the existing literature, for example, there is little close analysis of exactly how – and the extent to which – criminal careers and illicit drug careers can become a central element in shaping exclusionary transitions.

Defining 'social exclusion' is difficult. Commentators use different definitions and sometimes offer none at all. Its vagueness and elasticity has been recognised as a major problem in applying the concept in social scientific research (Hills et al, 2002). Ruth Levitas (1998) offers a convincing critique of the term and identifies several, competing ways of talking and thinking about it. Government policy usually stresses the social exclusion of people because of their lack of paid employment. Other approaches emphasise the importance of helping the poor through redistributing wealth. Finally, descriptions of the socially excluded 'underclass' sometimes suggest that the socially excluded – and their alleged 'cultures of poverty' – are responsible for their own predicament.

The most valuable recent approaches to understanding social exclusion stress the way that the *multiple problems* and *processes* of social exclusion interrelate and work over time to create populations and places of concentrated disadvantage (Bryne, 1999; Hills et al, 2002). Our study draws pragmatically on some of these insights and – through detailed, qualitative, longitudinal research – attempts to better understand what 'social exclusion' means for young adults living in a place said to be experiencing it in extreme form.

Research aims

The key research question suggested by our previous studies is where transitions that were varied, but in all cases economically marginal, *led* individuals in their mid- to late-twenties? The aims of this project, then, were to:

- chart the longer-term transitions and outcomes of young adults who had grown up in a context of social exclusion, as they reached their mid- to late-twenties;
- understand the key influences on social inclusion and exclusion for this age group, with particular emphasis upon the factors that affect engagement, disengagement and re-engagement with 'mainstream' and 'alternative' goals, activities and lifestyles;
- examine, to this end, extended participation in 'education, training and employment careers', 'extended family careers', and 'extended criminal and drug-using careers';
- draw out the implications for policy and practice interventions regarding longer-term

social inclusion and exclusion in poor neighbourhoods.

Research methodology

In order to achieve these aims, the current project followed up a sample of people selected from a merger of the original samples of our two previous studies. It was decided to re-interview those who were now aged 23-29 years (60 of the combined previous ESRC and JRF samples fell into this age range). A theoretical sampling approach sought to understand what the original studies suggested were particularly interesting types of transition, in a focused manner. Three different sorts of transition were identified, generating three sub samples that included people whose identities and energies, *when we last interviewed them*, were chiefly invested in these different sorts of transition. We planned to interview 10 people in each of the following categories.

- The *'education, training and employment sub-sample'* contained individuals who displayed enduring commitment to education, training and employment, even if their immediate post-school transitions were marked by economic marginality and instability.
- The *'family sub-sample'* consisted of individuals whose primary activity when we last interviewed them was parenting (predictably these were predominantly young women, many of whom were lone parents).
- The *'criminal/drug-using sub-sample'* was made up of young men and women who had displayed long-term criminal and/or dependent drug-using careers at the time of the previous studies.

These are analytic categories which are not mutually exclusive (for example, it was feasible, but in our experience unlikely in this context, that an individual might simultaneously have extended commitment to education and to dependent drug use). The study of these sub-samples does, however, help us focus on some of those processes of transition most likely to lead individuals to the wrong side of the 'youth divide' (Jones, 2002). As such, they help us to address some of the most pressing academic and policy debates about extended transitions and social inclusion/exclusion.

As expected, finding and accessing the 'new' sample was challenging. Ultimately in-depth interviews with 34 people were completed between February and July 2003: 11 in the 'education, training and employment sub-sample' (a third of those eligible for this particular sub-sample from the previous studies), 11 in the 'family sub-sample' and 12 in the 'criminal/drug-user sub-sample' (over half of those eligible for these two particular sub-samples from the previous studies). All sample members were white except for one of mixed British and Pakistani parentage, and there were 18 females and 16 males (see the Appendix).

Continuity and change in the extended transitions of socially excluded young adults

In this section, discussion of each of the three sub-samples begins with an individual cameo. Although each interviewee's story is unique, these three cases were selected because they are able to represent some of the most common experiences of others in each sub-group. We present a shortened version of each of their 'life grids', based on our interviews with them in the previous studies and this one. These map continuities and key changes by age in respect of the six career lines we studied. For presentation purposes we have conflated family and housing career – and drug-using and criminal career – in one column each. Following each cameo, we begin a more concerted effort to identify and understand similarities and differences across the three sub-samples.

The focus in each of the following three sections is on the young people selected on account of their main commitment to education, training and employment, or family and childcare responsibilities, or criminality and/or dependent drug use, at the time of their interview for the previous studies.

The 'education, training and employment' sub-sample

The persistence of economic marginality

Simon was first interviewed when he was 19, as part of the previous ESRC study. He had "hated" school, regularly truanted in order to escape severe bullying and left school – "the happiest time of my life" – with five GCSEs at low grades. At this time he had few friends and kept himself apart from offending peer groups who hung around the streets. His post-school career was typical of many: various low-paid, casual, service sector jobs were interspersed with spates of unemployment. Despite his early negative experiences of school, he returned to college on a part-time basis to improve his GCSE grades. At 19 he was unemployed for a year and was offered a 12-week work placement at the Nissan motor company through the NDYP programme. Despite his hopes he was not kept on, but soon after found a job as a factory operative with which he was "quite happy". He was then sacked from this factory job for reasons he considered "unfair dismissal" (an incident with the manager), became unemployed again and "absolutely sick of it". He abandoned a plan hatched with his friend to move to Northampton, to work in a supermarket, because the promised accommodation had fallen through. Although he had a girlfriend, he saw his future at the time of the first interview as being without a wife and children.

When we met him for this study, Simon was 23 years old. He continued to live with his close family – of parents, sister and grandparents – but now in "a better area" of Kelby (he had had his car stolen at the previous address and often stayed in to guard the house against burglary). He appreciated the financial and emotional support his family offered: "Basically, I love them, I can't fault them. If I'm having any trouble with money, then I can always ask 'em for a loan and all and stuff like that". He also now had a serious girlfriend, a relationship which he says has made him feel "a bit wiser". He hopes to move in with her and would like children "when financially secure". His social networks have become even more narrow than in his teenage years, restricted to his family, girlfriend and one or two best friends.

The education, training and employment career described in the first study was much the same three years later. Following various temporary jobs he got a permanent one, paying £185 per week, at a food-processing factory. He worked there for 12 months but resigned, saying "I'd been on permanent nights for a year. I was run down and I was drained out and thought I can't do it any more. So I put my notice in". Soon after he started a three-month, temporary job on the assembly line of a local electronics company. Again, a short period of unemployment led to his current, full-time job as a machine operative in a factory for which he received £150 per week. His plan, though, was to apply for a bus driver job: "£5.50 per hour is decent money". (See Table 2.)

Labour market precariousness

Virtually all our whole sample of 34 interviewees expressed strong commitments and aspirations to work, even if sustained engagement with the labour market had, for young mothers, been put on hold by the demands of parenthood or, for others, been overwritten by the attractions of criminality and drug use. One might have expected, however, that those who at first interview seemed closest to the labour market – 'the education, training and employment sub-sample' – might have had more 'success' in securing decent employment in the longer term.

Those in this sub-sample, however – and, indeed, all our interviewees – had difficult, extended transitions to paid employment. Those who had accessed jobs often described them as being poor quality, temporary and exploitative. Employment was usually intermittent and low-waged. One of our most striking findings is the durability of these informants' strong attachment to work, and the persistence of their search for it, in contexts where their aspirations were rarely met. While several individuals talked about enjoying particular jobs or work placements, most recognised that their experiences had been of 'dead-end' jobs that did not lead to career progression.

Simon's cameo (Table 2) contains many features that resonate with the experiences of the majority within the 'education, training and employment' sub-sample. Similar patterns of constraint, opportunity and continuity could be found in most of these cases. Poor school performance followed by various attempts to enter and establish oneself in decent, secure employment was met with frustration and anxiety.

For instance, Adam (now aged 25) had visited the Careers Service every week between the ages of 16 and 18 to no avail. Unable to find a job, he participated in youth training (YT) schemes. However, these were followed only by intermittent employment of low quality. Like others, he was frustrated by the lack of opportunity to prove his worth. Rejection letters cited his youth and lack of work experience: "It's just what's on that piece of paper [the application form] and they [employers] look at it and they say 'Do we want him or don't we want him?' That piece of paper holds me back". Of course, a *lengthening* record of marginal employment and intermittent unemployment is likely to mean an individual becomes even *less* attractive to employers as the years pass (Furlong et al, 2003). Adam started to feel disillusioned and began to worry that "there's no decent work out there". Eventually, at the age of 21, he started a New Deal retail placement and associated National Vocational Qualification (NVQ), which he "loved". At this time, and later, his hopes of securing relatively permanent jobs in music shops in the town were dashed because of new management and cost cutting. Looking back over his post-school labour market experiences, Adam described a 'cyclical' educational, training and employment career comprised of frequent movements between government training programmes, short-term retail jobs and long spells of unemployment, which he "despised". He was now once again unemployed but "desperately" looking for a new job.

Table 2: School-to-work sub-sample; Name: Simon; Age: 23

Age	Education, training and employment	Family and housing	Leisure and social networks	Crime and drug use
<13	"Hated" school	Living in parental home with mother, father and sister.	"Kept myself to myself". One best friend.	No crime
14-16	*Severely bullied, frequent truant.* five GCSEs (E and F grades): leaving was "happiest day of my life".	Ditto	*No 'street corner' socialising* – "daft".	Ditto
17-19	PT FE course in motor mechanics, NVQs 1 and 2 but left after 12+ months, disagreement with tutor. Unemployed (two weeks). PT cleaning job (eight months). PT fast food job at Butlins (one week). *Unemployed* (12 months).	Ditto Sister marries and moves out of family home. *Sees future 'on own', without wife or kids* – getting fed up with girlfriend. Would like 'peace and quiet' of countryside. Promised flat 'falls through' – returns to East Kelby.	New friend gets him interested in mechanics. Friend tells him of cleaning job. Friend encourages him to apply to Butlins. Weekday evenings – watches TV. Weekends – babysits with friend.	Ditto Starts occasional drinking. Some recreational cannabis use, for a few months – discontinues.
20-21	*Unemployed.* Various courses (eg Health and Safety) ... 'passing the time'. Informal learning (eg, computer skills). Begins accessing jobs via employment agencies. FT job food processing factory (12 months); *resigned.*	Ditto Still living with parents in East Kelby. Moves to different part of East Kelby – better; "no trouble". *Met girlfriend at work ("a big influence on my life now ... grown up a bit, a little bit wiser now").* Continuing strong relationships with parents, sister and grandfather.	Previous best friend moves to S. England. Happy to be more distant from ex-school peers. Networks of friends even tighter than teenage years ... social/leisure life conducted 'at home' with one or two 'best friends', girlfriend and family. Internet chat rooms/ creative writing.	No crime – odd speeding convictions only. No drug consumption, beyond occasional drinking. Crime "doesn't appeal to me"; 'respectable' working-class attitude. No holidays – "left at home to watch the house". Aware of local drug outlets.
22-23	Temp job on Samsung production line (three months). Temp job at Niffco (few weeks). FT job at Crest Hills (machine operative, three weeks to date; £150 pw). Goal: applying for bus driver job; "£5.50 ph is decent money".	*Continued dependence on family*; no 'board' paid. Would like kids "when financially secure", not yet. Future: "own house the next step, getting too old to live with mum and dad" – possibly move in with girlfriend.	Ditto Occasional carpet bowls and snooker outings. Bus driver job tip-off via best friend's dad.	Victim of car crime. Stopped attempted burglary at neighbours.

Poor work

Poor work conditions and often exploitative and punitive employers accompanied low-waged work (Brown and Scase, 1991). Alex, 25, resigned from her job as a sales assistant in a budget shop because:

"The Supervisor wasn't doing her job properly and leaving me to do it all, so when I said something to the Manageress about it, she started being funny with me and nasty and things like that."

She subsequently worked as a care assistant in a residential home for older people. Alex described the unsociable shift systems this entailed:

"I only have a Monday off and then I've gotta do everything on a Monday ... get things paid and go to the town if I need anything.... I start at seven most mornings. Then I come back home, after I've been to see people with my job [visiting older people as a carer]. I come back home about half past eleven, go back out, come back in about two o'clock and then go back out for about three. And I come back home and then I go back on a night."

As in our previous studies, the working conditions of care assistants seemed particularly miserable. Elizabeth, for instance, was so shocked by the conditions of employment in one care home – for example, on arriving for her first night shift she found herself the only member of staff present – that she quit this job, despite her long-held ambitions to be a care worker. Later she found alternative, stop-gap employment as a machine operative in a knitwear factory, working nine-hour shifts on £3.17 per hour. By the time of her most recent interview she had given up her plan to apply for nurse training because she had become accustomed to the wages factory work brought and enjoyed the company of her work-mates:

"[When] I went to the factory, I thought, 'Right, I'm gonna get a job I'm gonna hate'. Like in a factory, I thought I'd hate that and I'm gonna stay there until I start nursing. I thought if I hate the job, I'm gonna wanna leave to do nursing, but I got used to the money and the people and I didn't wanna

leave once I was in there. So nursing went down the drain."

These and other cases were typical of labour market experiences characterised by poor training, low-income jobs and periods of unemployment. Unsuccessful efforts to break into more secure or rewarding employment, as in Elizabeth's encounters with care work, could eventually lead to the further 'cooling down' of previous, modest ambitions. Interviewees' common experiences of these sorts of cyclical education, training and employment careers sometimes had an impact upon their willingness to think about forward planning in other spheres of their lives. In Adam's case, he wondered whether there was any point in thinking through long-term goals to the extent of his not wanting to settle into a long-term relationship, nor wanting children.

Improving employment prospects?

Earlier disaffection and disengagement from school did not wholly predict long-term refusal to re-engage in learning. The majority of the sample, as a whole, had had some further involvement with education or training courses since we last interviewed them. While three had accessed undergraduate university degrees (of which more later), the majority experience was of relatively short-term, basic courses that led to certificates in, for instance, first aid, introductory word processing, and health and safety and/or vocational training courses leading to NVQs. Many enjoyed vocational learning and these experiences may have brought other personal benefits. Overall, though, there was little evidence that participation in training schemes, further education courses and work preparation programmes – and the qualifications they gained – helped their chances of getting and staying in rewarding, secure jobs (Furlong, 1992).

Thus, the 'education, training and employment' sub-sample remained recurrently engaged with courses designed to help them into work. Many had repeated episodes of training. Several had experienced YT schemes, double doses of the NDYP and/or gained further qualifications (usually NVQs) post-school, but were now unemployed again. In general, informants spoke in negative terms about those interventions meant to improve their transitions into and through the labour market. Roy said of the NDYP: "They can't put me on a job that I don't wanna do. I wanna job that I like and I wanna do." Our previous studies showed that even where individuals had a more committed attitude to New Deal, and enjoyed the actual experience of it, little labour market benefit was observable (MacDonald and Marsh, 2005), as in Simon's encounters with his Nissan New Deal placement. After participating in the NDYP twice, Chrissie observed that "At the moment I'm suffering from depression because I've applied for jobs and then you just don't get them and so you just start feeling down."

The apparent ineffectiveness of schemes, programmes, courses and qualifications in helping our interviewees to get jobs did not result in their becoming wholly detached from the labour market. On the contrary, while unemployment was a common, recurrent feature of the sample's lives, so was employment (albeit in the form of poor work). Our earlier finding, that those who got jobs typically got them through tip-offs and informal recommendations from members of their social networks, was borne out again in this study. This experience of what was valuable in searching for jobs (that is, 'who you know, not what you know') served, in some cases, to confirm earlier, dismissive attitudes towards the relevance of qualifications in particular and education in general. As we describe later, Martin was one of the 'success' stories but he said "I've got a relaxed attitude to qualifications which I shouldn't really have". Roy was unemployed but mentioned some cash-in-hand, 'fiddly' work he had completed and how his friends:

"... try and help me get work ... someone phoned one of my friends and said 'Is there any chance you can get someone to come and work for us with you?' He come round to ask me straight away, 'cos he knew I was out of work."

This reliance on informal methods for seeking work through local social networks has important ramifications for the longer-term employment possibilities of the sample, which we discuss later, in Chapter 4.

More 'successful' employment experiences

The notion of a 'successful' transition to employment is problematic. For example, those whom we might classify as successful in this context might not be classified as such in more buoyant labour markets, or in comparison with more affluent cohorts of young people. Nevertheless, three of the 11 cases in our 'education, training and employment' sub-sample had experiences of more secure employment and/or of more advanced education that set them apart from the rest of the sample. While we need to be wary about taking these cases as in any way typical (they were unusually successful even compared with the larger samples studied in our original projects), they do allow us to scrutinise those factors that seem to generate more successful experiences of employment and education. We describe two of these cases below, before returning to the third in the concluding sections of this report, to assess their significance in understanding extended processes of social inclusion/exclusion.

Our first example of a more 'successful' transition to employment involves an agency that helps socially excluded young people. Martin had a patchy start. His school performance was poor, partly due to health problems. He then studied for NVQs in Business Administration and got an 18-month, temporary job at British Telecom (he unsuccessfully attempted to be made permanent). Martin eventually, however, got a job as a 'Business Support Officer' in an agency that helped NDYP participants set up in business. Now aged 23, he had worked for the same employer for four years and had gradually worked his way up the internal career ladder. He very much enjoyed this job and regarded his employer as supportive (for example, after the death of his first child; see Chapter 3).

Our second 'successful' case, Annie, showed how some individuals, despite unpromising earlier experiences, still managed to access higher education. She was the only one in the study to have gained a university degree (Marje, see Chapter 5, was still studying part-time and Sarah, whom we discuss in more detail when we turn to the 'family' sub-sample, had dropped out of university). Annie's earlier life experiences replicated those of others in the research and did not suggest that she would reach higher education. These were experiences of childhood bereavement (the death of her brother), long-term parental unemployment, frequent school truancy, leaving at 16 with no GCSEs and moving on to low-waged, temporary employment in care homes. While working in one of these she overheard a colleague talking about university Access courses and immediately enquired about joining one.

At the time of the first interview, aged 24, she had completed the Access course and started a degree course, but she reported that "I'm struggling like mad with money ... I can understand why people pack in for financial reasons". If perhaps the main, this was not the only pressure Annie faced. Her boyfriend wanted to start a family and had turned violent towards her, her family felt the debt 'wasn't worth it', she was ill-prepared for academic study, her fellow students were unsupportive and she juggled part-time care work with her studies. At 27, when we interviewed her again, she had graduated with an honours degree: "I was, like, 'Oh I'm never going to do it' but I stuck at it and I done it". She was currently not working because she was expecting the birth of her first child, after an unplanned pregnancy. She was confident about finding employment after her 'maternity leave', perhaps with one of the care homes where she had worked while studying for her degree. She had also thought about applying for a job in the police service. Given the relative scarcity of graduate employment in Kelby and the increasing numbers of people who possess degrees, we are unsure about predicting the likely labour market dividend provided by a university education, especially for 'non-traditional' students like Annie, who are likely to remain living in this locality. As Jones (2002) notes, "... the earnings and status value of a degree is likely to continue to reduce, and student debt increase, as more young people stay on". We return to this question in Chapter 4.

Summary: the 'education, training and employment' sub-sample

One might have predicted that those in the 'education, training and employment' sub-sample would be those most likely to have shown personal advancement in the labour market. While three were relatively successful, most continued to experience a cyclical pattern of precarious engagement with poor work,

unemployment, and various schemes and programmes. This is a pattern similar to that revealed in recent research on poorly qualified and socially disadvantaged young adults in Scotland (Furlong et al, 2003) and in other parts of north east England (Dolton et al, 2002). Young men and women whose consistent aspiration was to acquire decent work continued to circulate around the bottom of the labour market, moving in and out of poor work and unemployment. Although there was considerable further engagement with training schemes and college courses, these continued to be experienced as short-term, often unfinished and – in most cases – seemingly ineffective in progressing work careers.

Most of the education, training and employment careers that were described to us, across the sample, were redolent of economic marginality. This lack of progression to more secure, rewarding and remunerative employment had ramifications in other aspects of people's lives (for instance, as we will describe in Chapter 3, interviewees had to rely on state welfare and social housing in the movement to independent living and had notably impoverished leisure experiences). Although all informants had similar levels of educational qualifications, and struggled to make progress in the same labour market, a few fared better than the rest. An important key to relatively 'successful' transitions was having a good employer, as Martin's case shows.

Changes in other aspects of people's lives could also have ramifications for their education, training and employment careers. Three people in this sub-sample had or were about to become mothers since their first interview. For Carol-Anne and Annie, their new family careers meant engagement with the labour market was put on hold. Marje was the exception. She continued with her job and part-time study, alongside managing the demands of parenthood. She noted the challenge this entailed: "It's a balance with me home life, work, studying. It's not that I find the work hard, I find the juggling quite hard."

The 'family' sub-sample

The continuing priority of parenting

Nicky's early transition was straightforward. She spent her childhood in what she describes as a relatively comfortable situation compared with others around her ... this she put down to her mother meeting her step-father because "he had a good job and ... we got things like a TV in our room". Claiming to have "loved" school, Nicky and her friends were mischievous but she noted how "we still worked but we had a bit of a laugh in-between." Having gained eight GCSEs, Nicky went to college to do a childcare course before "going from job to job really". If she had not become pregnant at 19 it seems likely that she would have continued to follow a cyclical pattern of low-income jobs into her twenties. When first interviewed, she had a two-year-old boy and was unemployed but working four hours a week in a shoe shop "so I don't lose any [benefit] money and I get an extra £60 a month". She split with the father of her first child who already had two children from another relationship: "It got on my nerves him coming in and out all the time, so in the end I just shut the door".

At the time of first interview Nicky "definitely" wanted to get back to work full-time, aspiring to become a deputy manager in a shoe shop. She was interested in doing NVQ levels 3 and 4 in retailing. She also claimed "I don't want no more kids". By the time she was interviewed a second time, however, Nicky had a second child and was considering having a third. She was living in the same house – "close to our Mam" – with her new partner (the father of her second child) and wanted to marry him. Since meeting him Nicky claimed to have "experienced something I've never had before ... the closeness with another person" and her attitudes to family life had changed. She enjoyed being part of a "family unit". Her second child was not planned but she was clear that "I'd rather [he] gets the benefit of me, rather than me going back to work. I'd rather be out of pocket ... than him [son] suffer." But Nicky eventually wanted to return to employment once her youngest child started nursery and settled in – "... because I think I'd crack up ... I don't think I like the housewife thing. I like my house to be clean and tidy and stuff, but you do get sick of doing the same thing every day."

Nicky enjoyed the status of parenthood but being a parent was "hard". She felt more practical support could have been given, especially in the area of Kelby where she lived: "There's no crèches, or there's no mothers and toddlers [groups]". Her social networks became tighter and leisure time revolved around her children and her closest friends who were also mothers. Financial restrictions continued to shape her leisure time: "I miss it all but it's having the money ... if we're gonna spend £40 or £50 on a night out ... then I panic and think, 'what if a bill comes the next day?'" Despite moving around with her mother earlier in her life, Nicky had lived in the same house for several years. She was thinking of buying it last year but uncertainty regarding her, and her partner's, income meant that the risk involved was off-putting: "The fact of losing the house would be devastating". (See Table 3.)

Extended family careers: growing families, decision making and changing family roles

At the time of their most recent interviews all the 11 women in this sub-sample continued to place a primacy on their family career. Despite the overall pattern of continuity, however, it was possible to map some changes in respect of the size and constitution of family units (for example, new children, separations, new partners) and in the way that day-to-day family life was perceived and organised. As we will show, the fact that their children were now older has meant that, for some, other dimensions of transition have become more important.

Ten of the 11 women in this sub-sample had their first child as a teenager. The majority (seven) had one further child between first and second interview and one other had twins (ironically she learnt that this was going to happen when she went to be sterilised). Decisions to have more children or not were never reported as being easy ones. Complicated, angst-ridden balancing of difficult options was not uncommon. The financial costs of parenthood were often to the fore in these calculations and were a main factor, along with changing relations with partners, in explaining the abortions that some women had had since we first met them.

Table 3: Family sub-sample; Name: Nicky; Age: 25

Age	Education, training and employment	Family and housing	Leisure and social networks	Crime and drug use
<13	*"Loved"* school – latter run by nuns and very strict. Nicky is systematically *bullied* until confronts tormenter when returning from school.	Lives with mother and older brother until step-father joins them when Nicky is aged 9. Natural father left mother when Nicky was 3 years old – no further contact. Mother has further child to new husband – half-brother for Nicky.	Does not make many friends when moving to Willowdene – makes one who gets leukaemia who moves away. Nicky still feels a sense of *loss* years later.	Knows children who sniffed lighter gas resulting in one fatality. Everything *burgled* from house.
14-16	Plays tricks on teachers and finds it funny. Obtains 8 GCSEs – various low grades.	Mother goes to school when Nicky is in trouble and gives her "a clip" when she comes out. Moves to Willowfields with family.	Ditto	Caught smoking at school. Others in her year expelled for drug use. Home in Willowfields *burgled* three times.
17-19	Left school and did childcare course. Bunked off college and got "smacked in the face" by mother. Works in photo shop, then newsagents, then shoe shop. Leaves after criticism about her work. NVQ Retail levels 1 and 2 and then started at another shoe shop.	Brother goes to university. Aged 18 – moves into own house in Willowfields – rents from the council. Mother "five minutes away". *At 19 becomes pregnant* to a man of 30 she has been dating for 18 months. Separates from this man following birth of first child.	On hearing that Nicky is pregnant her older brother stops speaking to her for a while. However, offers a great deal of *support* once the child is born.	No crime or drug use
20-23	*Childcare costs and demands prevent her from working full-time –* continues to work one day a week in shoe shop. Aged 21 – becomes *pregnant again* and leaves part-time work in shoe shop.	Meets new partner and gets *engaged*. Aged 22 – birth of second child.	Friends from secondary school remain important. *Tighter network built around partner and childcare* – not much contact with five/six friends mentioned at first interview.	Ditto
24-25	*Unemployed* – receives Child Tax Credit and Working Tax Credit (partner works in a pizza shop).	Improved relations with parents – less "inter-ference" in her rearing of the children. Strong attachment to older brother (now married) – "he sort of acted like a father figure". Wants another child but partner "is not sure yet". No plans to move house – "knows everybody".	Restricted leisure pursuits – "It's having the money and then it's getting the kids minded".	Ditto

For instance, Sarah terminated a pregnancy after getting together with a new boyfriend who had started to take responsibility for her two older children. She said "[He] didn't want a baby. He'd just, like, had them two to look after and he was 'Ooh!' So we just thought it was the best thing to do." Despite recognising the "astronomical" childcare costs of having a third child, Tara decided to continue with her pregnancy. This was despite the fact that her husband had insisted she have an abortion (he attributed his own parents' divorce to the strain of looking after three children). Tara now felt the birth of her third child persuaded her partner of the wisdom of her decision.

Taking steps to prevent pregnancies was also evident. Charlotte and her partner did not want any more children and he had a vasectomy because, as Charlotte explained, "They're too much to look after and to give them a decent upbringing on the money that we have, because we haven't got no money". After a series of miscarriages Linda was sterilised:

"I could've miscarried. I could've had babies and if I'd have carried on to have kids, I'd have wanted a girl and every time I'd have had a boy, it'd have been heartbreaking. So I wouldn't have carried on because it would be more tears than happiness."

Over the period since we last interviewed them, the women in the 'family' sub-sample continued to take the main responsibility for childcare, family management and domestic work (regardless of whether they were living with a partner or whether they were employed or unemployed). Beliefs about what the 11 mothers felt their role should be within a household were varied. Some held more traditional views while others held more egalitarian ones. Some held views that clashed with those of their partner and in one case this resulted in the relationship ending:

"He [her partner] wouldn't help me with the kids. Like, he'd come home from work and that was it. Where I was still washing at eight, nine o'clock on a night, and ironing and doing pots. And he thought he didn't have to help me do any of that, and I thought that he did.... If the kids ever went anywhere, it was always me that took 'em,

all of 'em. He just wouldn't take the kids out." (Sally)

The importance of childcare

Many of the parents, especially the mothers in the sample as a whole, talked about the constraints that having a child had placed on other aspects of their lives. Childcare networks were central to achieving a life balance for all the mothers in this sub-sample. This was not simply a work–life balance for those in paid employment, although this was important. Those parents who were not in paid employment also had similar problems in establishing a balance between childcare and other activities. In fact, the most negative comments about parenthood came from non-employed mothers who felt they needed more support but, because of family circumstances and present state childcare funding arrangements, were not in a position to receive it. Many mothers in the study described opportunities for childcare as being more important than employment opportunities. Given their lack of employment, income and their personal preferences, most used childcare that was informal and delivered through personal, localised networks of kin.

On a day-to-day basis and over time, family resources and support – when provided – appeared essential when living in disadvantage. Indeed, belonging to families on low incomes and constantly juggling a small weekly income, often with debts and rent being repaid weekly, makes such support indispensable and highly valued. This is reflected in housing careers where a major factor in decision making was the ability to remain close to families of origin (see Chapter 3). Thus, families are especially important in disadvantaged areas as they offer an important element in people's ability to cope with the socioeconomic disadvantage of their neighbourhoods. Family networks provided the means through which financial, social and emotional support could be transferred between generations (even if the money lent only amounted to modest sums). These family networks are also vital in terms of the flow of information that shapes individual opportunities in respect of childcare and employment:

"I rely on our Mam babysitting and stuff like that and me sister. I don't know what

I'd do without 'em and borrowing all the time off them. They're only round the corner so it's dead easy ... most of the jobs I've had I've got through people I know." (Sophie)

The mothers in the 'family' sub-sample continued to access close personal ties with family and friends, helping them to initiate self-help and mutual aid strategies with others and as a form of social security, socialising and support. Given the current 'childcare gap' here as elsewhere (Daycare Trust, 2003) – and the prohibitive cost of childcare – it is not surprising that all the mothers we interviewed put together complex arrangements for their children's care involving informal provision through family and friends. Informal childcare was central to these parents finding a balance in their lives between parenting, work and socialising. Even among those in jobs, informal arrangements were needed because these parents often had employment outside normal working hours when little formal childcare was available.

These arrangements could be precarious and the availability of informal childcare networks could not be taken for granted. Our interviews with young mothers suggested that family relationships change, involve continual re-negotiation and can sometimes be fragile. While each interviewee could give examples of support from their original families or those that they had formed (particularly from their mothers and partners), this was not predictable and could be intermittent; such ties can also be contested and constraining. Sarah commented that: "When I had the eldest [daughter], it was, like, 'It's your child. You look after it. You do this. You do that. You'll have to find somewhere else to live. We've had our kids, dah dah dah.'"

Several women were especially critical about the amount of support they received on becoming a parent. Tara summed up these concerns:

"I think if you're on your own, or ... a first time parent, it can be a nightmare. I think, because I've had the other two, I'm much more relaxed with [the youngest son] now. I know more ... more or less what I'm doing.... Whereas, I mean, especially with [the first born child], the first year ... I was just sort of 'what am I doing?' But there was

nowhere to, like, turn, other than my family ... which, if someone hasn't got that..."

Sure Start

It is parents like these that Sure Start was designed to help. It is targeted at the poorest areas of the country and three programmes currently cover the neighbourhoods where virtually all this sub-sample lived. Those mothers who attended Sure Start programmes were, on the whole, positive about them. Alice recalled how on becoming a parent she "felt like I had lost everything. I couldn't go nowhere. I couldn't do anything.... But I'm getting out all the time now. I'll go to Sure Start and I've got more things to do." Sally gave the most glowing report:

"... we just went to a fun day – that was last year. Me and me cousins and a friend up the road, we've been going to everything – about four times a week – they do training.... They're brilliant. There's always something on nearly every day so if you're fed up sitting in at home – I mean it's just up the road, we've got a brand new building ... we basically get what we want, as long as it's got something to do with education and your children's needs ... we're making, well it's going be better for the kids, innit? They're getting a better start in life."

The Chancellor of the Exchequer has called Sure Start 'the country's best kept secret' (Brown, 2003). Certainly several of the mothers we interviewed were unaware of the existence of Sure Start programmes in their locality or did not know what services they offered (note Nicky's comments in her cameo (p 11) about the lack of crèches in her area). Tara had pre-school age children but struggled to explain how Sure Start might help her: "It's one of those things, I've heard the name of it but I've never been able to find out exactly what it is ... it's a bit lost on me." Val lived close to a Sure Start scheme but had not heard of it. Yet it was clear from her interview that she might have appreciated some help with childcare: "Just to have somebody to take 'em and give me a little bit of time to myself".

These experiences seem to suggest some problems in the promotion and perception of

Sure Start programmes in these neighbourhoods. As we will discuss in Chapter 5, there are also concerns about the increasing emphasis that Sure Start is placing on the employability of young parents.

Relationships between parenting and education, training and employment

The previous studies found that many of the young mothers in the 'family' sub-sample were largely detached from employment. At the time of their most recent interview, this pattern was continuing for many. Only three of the eleven mothers were currently employed: one full-time (Tara as a hairdresser) and two part-time (Mary as a cleaner and Sophie as a chambermaid). Another, Sarah was participating in a work placement at a hospital under the NDYP programme. Two had not been employed at all since the first interview and the remaining five had only undertaken very short-lived jobs, lasting a week at most, as cleaners and shop assistants.

Because all the mothers had taken on the main role of bringing up their children, they had become separated from employment. Amy, for example, did only two days 'fiddly' work in a pizza shop between first and second interview. She had applied for several cleaning jobs but felt that employers "did not want to know" when they found out she had two children: "They get the impression that I'd rather be at home with them; perhaps I give them that impression". Those mothers who were not currently in paid employment all viewed this status as temporary and explained their decision in terms of the interests of their children. They regarded staying at home during their early upbringing as of central importance. For example, Nicky (presented in Table 3) felt that employment was not currently an option, despite the fact that her previous job, in a shoe shop, was apparently still open to her. Since the birth of her first child she had not been employed, nor had she completed any training (despite her earlier interest in training as a paediatric nurse). In short, Nicky felt that motherhood involved taking on full-time responsibility for childcare: "I wouldn't leave the kids with anybody". Linda had not had a job since her first interview, for the same reasons as Nicky: "I look after me kids; apart from me and me Mam and me Dad, nobody else has them.... I think it's my responsibility."

Mary and Sophie (both lone mothers) took paid employment once their children were older and suitable childcare arrangements were in place. Often the nature of this childcare restricted people's labour market options. Those who had free, *part-time* nursery provision limited their search for employment to *part-time* jobs. As Mary observed:

> "... it's convenient. It's not what I wanna do. It's not a great job, but it's convenient.... It's not, obviously, what I wanna do, but it's just across the road from [her son's] school and he starts at nine o'clock, finishes at half twelve, so ... it was perfect for what I needed at the time.... Especially to get [my son] used to me working. He just needed something to ease him in."

The one mother in this sub-sample who continued to work full-time after having children, Tara, said "I love going to work. I feel sanity away from baby talk." However, Tara qualified this statement by noting "If I ever had to give up work due to something with the kids, or with [my husband], then I'd have no qualms". She described her job as a hairdresser as a "break" from the demands of motherhood.

Only two of the mothers (Sarah and Sally) had received any formal education and training since their first interviews. At first interview, Sarah was doing a full-time degree course. She successfully completed two years – resitting one – before being forced to withdraw due to "financial" pressures. In comparison with Annie (from the 'education, training and employment' sub-sample who had successfully completed her degree but worked part-time while completing it), Sarah had two children. Friends and family cared for Sarah's children while she attended college, but she was unable to take on part-time jobs to help ease her financial burden of studying full-time. She was currently on NDYP placement in a hospital and questioned the value of education: "Unless you're going into a profession like teaching, I don't think it gets you any further. I don't think people look at things like that." Sally had completed several beauty therapy courses at a local further education college and through Sure Start, and was planning to become a self-employed beautician once her younger children were older. She spoke very positively about Sure Start: "I think Sure Start's been the biggest impact. I've got loads of confidence. I wanted to go back to college and everyone was always, 'next time, next time'. And just by going to Sure Start … and I thought, 'Yeah, I can go to college, and I can do it.'"

So across the 'family' sub-sample the roles and responsibilities associated with family careers clearly had a curtailing effect on labour market participation. One might interpret this as choice: in most cases the mothers in our study attached more personal importance to the rewards of staying at home to care for children than they did to employment. One also needs to consider the context in which such a choice is made. Like virtually all the other men and women in this study, these young parents were firmly located in a secondary segment of the labour market (Loveridge and Mok, 1975) marked by pervasive under-employment and unemployment, insecurity and poor work (see Chapter 4). In such contexts, pursuing the 'mothering option' (Craine, 1997) is, at least in part, reflective of the lack of opportunities for decent, rewarding employment for such women.

Summary: the 'family' sub-sample

In many respects the direction and nature of the transitions that these young mothers had been making when we first met them did much to influence their later biographies and life-chances as they moved through their mid-twenties. Longer-term patterns and degrees of social exclusion/inclusion were partly related to these early experiences. In particular, the ramifications of having children at an early age could be great (particularly in respect of detachment from the labour market). Across the 'family' sub-sample, parenthood brought a 'fast track' to adult status but attached to it were several roles and responsibilities that were very much characterised by gender inequality. These inequalities meant that the young women took on the greatest responsibility for domestic labour, household management and childcare duties in their households.

Opportunities for childcare were a preoccupation of all the mothers we interviewed regardless of whether or not they returned to paid employment after having children. Informal childcare was preferred and was important in terms of life balance, again regardless of whether

or not one was in employment. Informal childcare arrangements and networks were essential and, until they were ensured, women could not compete in the local labour market. Consequently, we conclude that local structures of opportunity in respect of education, training and employment do not on their own help us understand processes of transition and inclusion/exclusion for young parents, especially mothers. The availability of childcare arrangements that were durable, affordable and matched their personal preferences was crucial in understanding the broader and longer-term transitions of all the mothers we interviewed.

The 'criminal and/or drug-using' sub-sample

The evolution – and termination? – of criminal and drug-using careers

Micky had lived outside the law – literally an 'outlaw' – and had no significant contact with any formal institutions after leaving school aged 11, until he collided with the youth justice system at 14 and received his first custodial sentence at 15. His transition was marked by no or little engagement with education, training or the labour market, with social services or drug treatment services, with 'normal' leisure and consumption, with finance, banking or credit or with the housing market. His sole, enduring 'engagement' had been with the police, criminal justice system and prisons. All his experiences, apart from these, had been informal and within his immediate social networks. For these reasons it is difficult to tell Micky's story in the same way as we did with the cameos of Simon and Nicky earlier. His drug use and crime were, in a sense, the whole story.

At first interview, aged 21, Micky described a pattern that included early persistent truancy; anti-school and disruptive behaviour; active attempts to get school suspension; early association with a similarly disruptive but older friendship group; the ineffectiveness of family or school to control his behaviour; early abandonment of school; involvement with recreational but heavy use of alcohol and drugs (financed through increasingly persistent and serious acquisitive crime); further embeddedness in a drug-using, criminal social network; and eventual heroin use at the age of 18. Offending escalated to fund a £100 a day heroin habit, graduating from what had been a £40 a day alcohol and cannabis habit.

The defining feature of his transition was a drug-fuelled criminality based on chronic heroin dependency interspersed with prison and then chronic relapse. Yet he positioned himself as a heroin user in particular ways. He described himself as a smoker not an intravenous user – a "drug user" not a "bag 'ead" – thus actively avoiding a certain heroin-using self-identity. Avoiding any drug treatment, even in prison, was cited as a counterpoint to a 'smackhead' identity. His 'enforced' detoxifications were self-managed without medication or counselling. It is difficult to envisage how formal controls or interventions might have relevance in the lives of career criminals and drug users like Micky, other than in the containment provided by prison.

Micky's account of his life spoke of the influence of loss and grief and bereavement as touchstones of personal experience: the tragic loss of his sister and friends in a car crash, his mother through illness and his care for an ailing father. At the time of his recent interview, Micky was attempting to keep away from crime and heroin use and had done so over the four months since he had been released from prison on bail. Since his first interview a number of key turning points had occurred in Micky's life. He regarded the deaths of his sister and friends, in 1999, as responsible for his return to heroin addiction. As a result of this return to crime and prisons he had reluctantly finished with a long-standing partner. In the previous four years his family had abandoned him at certain times because of his heroin use. He increasingly regretted this. In addition, his social network had diffused because of the heroin use and serial imprisonment of its members. Accompanying the decline of his social network, he was committed to a new 'clean' partner and her family. Before his mother died of cancer, he promised her that he would never use heroin again. Promises to his mother and partner to 'stay clean' seemed defining moments in Micky's struggle to avoid chronic relapse. (See Table 4.)

Understanding criminal and drug-using careers: different processes and outcomes

Our previous studies noted how a cheap and plentiful local heroin market had become embedded in Kelby in the mid-1990s. Before then the town had little appreciable history of heroin use (Parker et al, 1988). Once a market was established, informal knowledge about use was passed from experienced users to novices (Parker et al, 2001, p 6) and a complex network of dealers and users was created. This localised drug market had affected most, if not all, of the young people living in our research sites in some way. Virtually every interviewee held strong, negative views about the prevalence of heroin and drug-related crime within the estates where they lived.

Except for those in this sub-sample, no other interviewees displayed – currently or previously – drug or offending behaviour that would normally be regarded as problematic or which had longer-term influences on their transitions. Several interviewees across the whole sample *had*, for instance, used cannabis *recreationally* in the past. Some continued to do so but there was also evidence that this recreational use was declining with age. Some of the young mothers, for instance, described how they had stopped using recreational drugs with the onset of the responsibilities of parenthood.

This section outlines – at an individual, case-by-case level – the processes of decision making that constitute more committed criminal and/or drug-using careers and their implications. Particular attention is devoted to how such careers are influenced by local neighbourhood social structures made up of particular kinds of social, cultural and economic capital and defined by economic marginality and social exclusion (Bronfenbrenner, 1979; Sampson and Laub, 1993; Jones Finer and Nellis, 1998).

There were differences in respect of the criminal and drug involvement of the 12 individuals in this sub-sample and the following discussion attempts to identify these in order to better understand patterns of continuity and change.

Table 4: Criminal and/or drug-using sub-sample; Name: Micky; Age: 25

Age	Education, training and employment	Family and housing	Leisure and social networks	Crime and drug use
<13	"Hated" school and teachers – *stopped attending school altogether at 11 years old.*	Persistent but failed attempts by mother and Education Welfare Officers to enforce school attendance. Lives in family home with six sisters and two brothers.	Started hanging around with and being influenced by older peers. All night socialising.	Chronic alcohol abuse
14-16	*No aspirations* to gain employment. *No engagement* with training or the job market.	Ditto	"Hanging around with the wrong people", ie, friendship group of six all sharing the same activities.	Chronic cannabis and alcohol use, glue sniffing. *A lot of low-level acquisitive crime (shoplifting) and 'twocking' (taking vehicle without consent).* Probation order and custodial sentence for 'twocking'.
17-19	Never signed on.	Mother and father continue attempts to dissuade from crime and drugs and threaten to end contact with Micky. 'Respectable' and criminal brothers. Unemployed parents. Father suffers chronic ill-health.	Friends begin serving prison sentences. After prison returns to friendships – same group. *Heroin use begins among whole group.*	*Heroin use begins* – custodial sentence for aggravated 'twocking', etc. *Offending escalates in frequency from shoplifting to shed burglary then house and shop burglary then robbery.* Curfew Order followed by custodial sentence for burglary
20-23	States a belief in the work ethic and meritocracy, and aspires to live in a "decent" place... *unemployed.* No help in finding employment.	Steady girlfriend of three years then split. Returned to family home. *Sister and two best friends killed in car accident.* Relationship to family deteriorates due to drug use.		Prison sentence for burglary, theft and handling. *Released from prison. Returned to heroin use and burglary, car crime etc, to fund drug-use.*
24-25	About to enter New Deal depending on outcome of trial.	Thrown out of family home several times. Visit while in prison by family friend who becomes partner. *Mother died while he was in prison.* Has bail address but lives with brother's girlfriend. Family relations return to being strongly supportive.	Seems to have abandoned primary peer group – one died in same car "accident" as his sister.	Custodial sentence. *Returned to offending* – custodial sentence for burglary – on bail. *Desisted from heroin use since mother died. Promise made to her and girlfriend to stay clean.* Continues chronic alcohol and cannabis use funded through dole and family loans. *Never received drug treatment except drug counselling in prison.*

Intravenous users versus heroin smokers

The seriousness and persistence of repeat offending crosscut with drug-using careers (of the 12, eight had been or were heroin users) varied within the sub-sample. Danny's career of persistent criminality was similar to that of Micky's, whom we presented in Table 4. It continued from the pattern observed in our first study; a pattern of early teenage truancy, school exclusion, children's homes, continuous unemployment and some 'fiddly' work. Both his and Micky's cases suggest that smoking, in contrast to intravenous heroin use, may help avoid the more debilitating effects of dependency, especially when use is interrupted by long spells in prison. Although not inhibiting criminality, smoking had meant that criminality was more independent of drug use, compared with the heroin-driven offending of some of the intravenous users.

Danny started smoking heroin in 1997 "just because it was there". All his friends were from his estate and were in and out of prison. Many of them quickly moved from smoking to injecting but he kept his distance from intravenous users, ending a relationship with a girlfriend because she was injecting heroin. He said, "That's no life for me, that". Interviewed for a second time at the age of 24, he was still unemployed and living in a town nearby to Kelby with his partner. They had a child and were about to marry. Having stopped using and offending at age 23, he cited as reasons for his desistance the birth of his daughter, childcare responsibilities, the discouragement of his partner, reconciliation with his family of origin, maturity, drug counselling and 'blockers' (that is, medication that blocks the effects of heroin). Comparing his life now with when he was first interviewed he said it was "totally different":

> "'Cos I was all over. I was never in one place before. I was always just ... always like out in a car [usually stolen] and taking drugs and committing crime 24 hours a day. Where now I'm just in the house all the time, or going up [his partner's] Mam's and helping out and that."

In terms of the future, Danny's problem was that he had a substantial criminal record so the only option, albeit a risky one, seemed some kind of self-employment. Earlier rejection by parents because of his drug use, in part, served to further isolate him in a drug-based world. In several cases like Danny's, later re-engagement with parents, siblings, partners and children seemed a key factor in enabling desistance. For Danny, enforced detoxification in prison, his release and a subsequent move to a different town to join his long-standing partner (thus facilitating his avoidance of previous, local criminal and drug-using social networks) also seemed necessary conditions for his rehabilitation.

Desisters

These processes and conditions, which were present in various and contrasting ways among the others, we describe as desisters. For instance, Richard's offending seemed wholly heroin-driven. A reluctant, intermittent, intravenous user from early stages of his drug career, he had maintained fuller engagement with employment and training than Danny or Micky, at least until heroin use caught up with him at the age of 20. He did not reveal his criminal record when applying for jobs and, post-16, he had obtained a series of labouring jobs and placements on government schemes as a fitter, butcher and scaffolder. His frequent school truancy, heavy cannabis use and brief spell of petty shoplifting in his early teens gave no indication, however, of what was to follow.

This included more concerted shoplifting and commercial burglary to fund his heroin addiction for which he was sentenced to a period in a Young Offender Institution (YOI). Ejected from his mother's home, he was intermittently homeless. After desisting from heroin use at various points while employed, he returned to heroin use again aged 19 when living at a homeless hostel where he again encountered other heroin users. Short periods of intensive and addictive heroin use brought on a spate of offending to fund it, followed again by custodial sentences, self-detoxification and chronic relapse. A year prior to the second interview he was released from a custodial sentence with a probation order for drug rehabilitation and had sought and been receiving a methadone maintenance programme at a local, specialist GP practice (which he described as "excellent"). While on the programme he was not using, avoided other users and lived with his partner. He also joined another scaffolding training scheme but was absent a great deal due to the demands of his methadone programme.

Like others, Richard cited the "vicious circle" of heroin use, offending, prison, and relapse to heroin use. His case also highlights the problems of attempting to escape a drug-using career that induced an 'every man for himself' situation. More often than not, the 'solution' appeared to be the influence of significant relationships with women counterposed to a life of criminality and drug use. Richard gave the reason he wanted to stay off heroin and succeed in his methadone treatment as "just to make me Mam happy at me and then having a normal life with me girlfriend, isn't it? Like everyone else does". He went on:

> "It's [heroin use and crime] like a vicious circle, I see it as. It's like one big magnetic, magnetic circle ... and when you get out of jail it starts, you're slowly getting drawn back in all the time ... slowly you end back on the circle again, moving round and round back in the same direction all the time."

Some of those who had *not* been heroin users but who, by the time of this study, were attempting to desist from criminal careers, had obtained jobs. Given the labour market fortunes of others in the sample, their 'success' in getting any sort of employment is surprising. Despite a troubled childhood, criminal father, hatred of school, alcohol abuse, persistent offending and a custodial sentence for serious assault at first interview, Broderick was now employed full-time as a scaffolder, earning £250 per week. Broderick had never been wholly detached from the labour market and, at first interview, had described the importance of informal local networks in getting the legitimate and 'fiddly' manual work he had done since school. He was now living with his partner and their young child, close to his family of origin. He said that many of his previous social network had "settled down" and he saw them less often than before, usually only on a weekend: "... 'cos a few of us are working and a couple of them have kids, so like Friday is when we meet up. If you see 'em during the week, you do 'Are you going out Friday?', 'Yeah', 'See you in the club.'"

Harry was another informant who had not used heroin but who was attempting to desist from crime. Like Broderick he was now attempting to settle into legitimate employment but his interview illustrated the economic logic of crime. Acquisitive offending can appear more attractive when the financial gains to be had seem much greater than those available from local, legitimate employment, especially when offending itself compounds exclusion from such opportunities. Harry had not offended since release from prison, six months prior to his second interview. He had stopped offending because his girlfriend became pregnant. Despite his partner wanting a child, they felt that they could not afford the costs and she had had an abortion. Harry regarded this as a turning point in his life. Although having been sacked previously from a factory job for the non-disclosure of his criminal record, he was currently employed at a call centre, on a probationary basis, and took home £900 per month. At the height of his criminal career, Harry estimated that he had been 'earning' around £30,000 per annum, several times that of his current salary and approximately double that of the highest, legitimate earner in our study. He said that: "... when you get caught you go into jail and you don't have to pay lodge, you don't have to work. Just sit on your arse and do nowt.... We had less worries when I was committing crimes."

When read alongside the others in this sub-sample, Harry's biographical account suggests a number of things. Having served 10 custodial sentences (excluding remands) between 1995 and 2002, prison does not appear to rehabilitate offenders (at least in Harry's case). Probation could only offer minimal support. A criminal record, if admitted, can in effect debar ex-offenders from legitimate employment, as can a probation hostel or bedsit address. Renting or taking out a mortgage on a house is difficult and borrowing is unlikely because of the lack of a credit history. The ability to move away from Teesside for employment or other reasons is thus curtailed. As Harry's comments below testify, this has serious ramifications for *education, training and employment careers*:

> "I started the job. I wasn't late once, I wasn't sick once ... erm, hadn't missed a shift.... And basically, when they found out I did have a [criminal] record, he shot us out the door without even an explanation.... I was more reliable than some of the people he had in there.... So, that's what bugs me."

For *housing careers*:

"I went for a house, a couple of month back. I was in full-time employment, erm … I hadn't committed a criminal offence since 2000, since my release. So that was, like, three year without an offence…. Basically, they said 'No, because of your list of offences'. I mean, I told them I had a criminal record. I volunteered all the information…. They just kept turning me down for a house. It's basically, no one wants to give you a chance. That's what I've come across."

And in respect of *family careers*:

"I mean, her [his partner's] Mam and Dad used to hate me. The first words I got out of her Mam's mouth were, when I seen her, were 'stay away from my daughter and my doorstep'. So, when we have a drink I always take the piss out of her with that…. They're all right now."

The cases we have discussed in this sub-section illustrate the important role played by processes of (re)engagement with family (with parents, siblings and new partners) in the attempts of individuals to desist from long-term criminal and drug-using careers. In some cases, employment also emerged as an important factor in attempts to establish more firmly complete cessation of offending.

Persisters

Some of our interviewees persisted in repeated offending into their mid-twenties and showed little signs of changing at the time of our current study. The cases of David and Jason demonstrate this point. An important finding, illustrated by some of our earlier examples, is that those who desisted from and those who persisted in crime had *similarly* troubled backgrounds, and that in both cases contingent life events influenced the course of their criminal and drug-using careers. In other words it would be difficult to explain, by reference to the earlier biographies of these individuals, why some continued with crime while others desisted.

Jason's early truancy, prolific drug use and offending, long-term health problems (some of which were drug-related), hospitalisation at 19 for a heroin overdose and little engagement with licit or illicit employment, fit the profile of a career criminal and drug user. At first interview, it was clear that his offending escalated after he began using heroin. At second interview he expressed little desire to stop offending and saw his drug use as only a partial reason for his offending, the main one being economic; far more money could be 'earned' from crime than legitimate employment.

Jason's main aim was to change his *type* of offending (from burglary and theft to drug-dealing) so as to ensure that crime was more lucrative and its risks reduced. Like David (discussed below), he had no relationship with his parents, conducted short-lived relationships with girlfriends, had no 'close' friends (knowing mostly only other drug users and criminals) and avoided drug treatment because of being stigmatised and labelled as a heroin user. He seemed socially isolated and resigned to his lifestyle. Like others, Jason cited the compounding effects of being a career criminal in reinforcing the "vicious circle" that worked against desistance:

"I've been in and out of prison for years and years and it gets to the point [where I think] 'I'm gonna stop this, I'm gonna go straight when I get out of here'. When you get out, you go straight back into the same area, same faces, all the drug users. So it's a vicious circle. You get straight back into things."

David had been a prolific offender and career criminal from early in his life. His biography spoke of loss: his mother abandoned him to care homes, his father left when he was young and his brother died. His long-standing institutionalisation in a string of care homes, secure units, YOIs and prisons made it difficult for him to form social relationships outside. It was difficult to discern what, if any, family or other relationships might discourage him from criminality and drug use (even though his own mother was currently caring for his young child).

Occasional offenders

We interviewed others with careers of more occasional offending. Two types of criminal career were apparent. First, there was earlier, relatively short-lived offending among non-dependent drug users. Here avoidance of drug use was accompanied by a strong anti-drugs ethos and relatively continuous orientation to the labour market.

Second, there was a pattern of low-level, sporadic offending to fund heroin habits followed by desistance helped by drug treatment (for example, methadone maintenance programmes). Among occasional offenders the influence of drug use on crime was less clear than that in respect of the more prolific offenders. In some cases, heroin use was the sole spur to – and had preceded – offending. Stopping drug use meant stopping offending. For most, however, there was a pattern of early truancy, 'hanging around' the public space of their neighbourhoods and petty offending *prior* to heroin use. Most wished to repair the earlier damage to family and personal relationships that had resulted from drug dependency, although this moral awareness did not often extend beyond family, friends and partners to the harm that had been caused by offending to other households and businesses.

It would be wrong to conclude that the life-courses of the occasional offenders were less troubled than those of persistent offenders and drug users. There was just as much evidence here of early family conflict, trauma and loss in their lives. Stuart, for example, had been arrested for the alleged rape of his sister when younger but the case was dropped. This resulted in his estrangement from his mother and sister: "She's [his sister] ruined my life. Can't talk much to people any more. You know, like, can't go out and meet people and that ... make conversations."

Summary: criminal and/or drug-using sub-sample

The most important 'predictors' of later desistance among criminals and dependent drug users were sustained employment, support from family of origin, forming a family and having children and support from a partner (often living outside the immediate local area). Support from a non-drug-using partner seemed particularly important for those desisting from dependent drug use, as was availability and knowledge of

good quality, non-punitive drug treatment services (although a few were able to stop using heroin through self-detoxification aided by partners). Several persistent offenders and drug users described a 'vicious circle' that involved a pattern of repeated episodes of drug dependency, offending, prison, enforced detoxification, chronic relapse into drug dependency, offending, prison and so on.

Paradoxically, for intravenous users custodial sentences often had the effect of permitting drug dependent careers to be extended for longer than might otherwise have been the case. Prison offered a moratorium from the debilitating health and social problems associated with longer-term, chronic heroin use. There was, however, evidence of self-detoxification among those who had *not* received custodial sentences (sometimes with support from family or partners). Those who, by second interview, had persisted in their offending and drug use seemed to lack any identifiable 'moral reference point' because of their isolation from 'significant other' relationships with family, non-criminal friends or partners. The amount of time they had spent in custody seemed to disqualify them from forming such relationships.

Despite attempts by several in this sub-sample to move their employment, family and housing careers forward in a positive direction, the consequences of earlier criminal careers (especially those enmeshed with a drug-using career) were significant. The metaphor of the 'vicious circle' goes some way to understanding the effects of heroin use on extended transitions. It does, however, imply that once out of the 'circle' (that is, becoming drug-free) the problem is resolved once and for all. Our evidence of repeated relapse suggests that this is not the case and that a metaphor of *'cork-screw' drug-crime careers* might be more apposite.

The more protracted the heroin career, the greater the tolerance, the greater the need for money to fund increased consumption and, therefore, the more prolific, desperate and serious the crime. Lengthening records of serious offending resulted in lengthening records of incarceration. Those caught up in these spiralling processes became ever more deeply embedded in destructive lifestyles and social networks organised around heroin use and ever more distanced from sources of support that might aid desistance. Eventually they reached 'the tip of the cork-screw', experiencing the most damaging, chaotic effects of their drug dependency. The "decision" to "get clean" and "go straight" is only the first step in a long, arduous, risk-laden struggle back to a "normal life", as Richard put it. This necessitates facing – and overcoming – the cumulative personal, social and economic consequences of their long-term careers of crime and drug use and explains why many in this sub-sample had biographies that were replete with instances of failed attempts at desistance (see Laub and Sampson, 2003).

3

Broader experiences of extended transitions

The previous section highlighted experiences of continuity and change in extended transitions that were particularly relevant to the three sub-samples we interviewed. This section will discuss those broader experiences and processes of transition that emerged as important in understanding the wider transitions and outcomes of *all* our interviewees.

The persistence of poverty

In some respects this study revealed considerable change in interviewees' lives since we last met them. The most obvious example of this is that a good proportion had made significant transitions in terms of their family and – as will be described later in this chapter – housing careers. Independent living and parenthood were new experiences for many. How a majority had desisted from problematic criminal and drug-using careers was also striking (although this apparent change must be understood as contingent, aspirational and fragile). Individuals reported feeling considerable *subjective* change in their lives that hinged around key turning points and critical moments, especially in respect of family, housing, criminal and drug-using careers.

That said, their *objective* circumstances in terms of employment and income had remained generally constant since our previous studies. Regardless of whether or not they were working, had established their own home or become parents, the majority experience of material poverty had persisted to the time of our most recent interviews. As noted in Chapter 2, extended educational, training and employment careers continued, in the main, to be marked by economic marginality and the rapid movement in

and out of insecure, low-paid, low-skilled work, training and employment preparation schemes and repeated spells of unemployment. Recurrent unemployment and low-paid work contributed to a high level of personal poverty across the *entire* sample.

Across the whole sample of 34, 10 people now worked in full-time jobs, two were participating in NDYP, 20 were registered as unemployed (two of whom did part-time work that did not affect their benefit entitlement) and two were imprisoned. As noted previously, young mothers were less likely to be in full-time jobs (and more likely to be unemployed), and that even a third of those with extended careers of crime and drug use were now in full-time, legitimate employment is perhaps surprising. There was relatively little difference, however, in the pay earned by people in these different sub-samples. Admittedly, the highest earners were Marje (£16k pa) and Martin (£12k pa), from the 'education, training and employment' sub-sample, but lower pay was common across the sample. Many quoted income around, and in one instance below, the level of the National Minimum Wage (at the time of the study this was £4.20 an hour, or £168 for a 40-hour week, for those aged over 22).

Overall the majority of informants appeared to be receiving income below or around that currently equated with poverty. This threshold is measured as 60% of medium income, which for the population as a whole was £187 per week before housing costs in 2002 (DWP, 2003). Living with a partner or parents can ease personal poverty and raise overall household income above the 60% poverty threshold. In our study, however, most parents and partners were also in low-paid work or unemployed, and therefore able to provide only modest financial assistance at best. Although all interviews contained discussions of the experience of continued poverty, those who were parents were most explicit about the problems of living in poverty. Linda's household income was entirely dependent on social security benefits. Her interview stressed the careful budgeting that was required to make ends meet:

"I think you manage. I think you work your money out and you manage on it. You sort of, like, think, 'Well I've got this'. Me bills are always paid. Once your bills are paid and your shopping's in and your gas and electricity there, you've got nothing else to worry about, so ... the kids are provided for."

Sally commented on the "expense" of six children "especially when all their other friends go to school and they've all got nice trainers. You try your best to get them the same." Like Linda, Sally and other young mothers, Charlotte couched her description of the day-to-day struggles to get by on benefits with reference to the effects on her children: "We have no money.... I have had things for the kids out of the charity shops but I wouldn't go in there all the time ... I wanna be able to buy my kids nice-looking things."

Recent rises in Child Benefit and the introduction of tax credits have provided a welcome boost to the incomes of some interviewees, particularly those who are parents. Our evidence suggests, however, that Child Benefit rises are marginal (and of course many members of the sample do not have children). Child Tax Credit was introduced in April 2003, during the course of our fieldwork. It is paid to designated parents (usually mothers) who care for children, regardless of whether or not they are in paid employment. Previously, tax credits were useless for most of the parents in our study because they could only be claimed if they and their partners were working 16 hours or more per week (which most were not).

Carol-Anne said "Like, we've been able to buy things and go shopping where we want and not have to worry. It's lovely." Receipt of tax credits also means, however, that parents lose other benefits such as entitlement to free school meals for their children. The cost of paying for these meals can negate the potential benefits accrued

from tax credits, as Nicky pointed out: "I pay for his [her oldest son's] dinners. Which is gonna be a nightmare when [her youngest son] goes to school."

Tax credits are meant to act as an incentive to get young mothers to return to the labour market. As discussed in Chapter 2, however, this runs counter to the preferences of many of the mothers in this study to stay at home to care for children. It also takes little account of the uneven spread of suitable opportunities in respect of childcare and employment and how, in places like Kelby, this can also constrain 'the return to work' of young mothers. Paid work may provide protection against family poverty but, to reiterate, the work undertaken by the majority in our study, whether parents or not, was of a type that failed to lift them clear of persistent poverty. We return to a fuller consideration of how and why objective conditions of poverty persist in Chapter 4, where we also try to understand how the subjective mainstream aspirations of poor people to 'better themselves' become reconciled with constrained socioeconomic conditions. In Chapter 5, we scrutinise further policies that are designed to tackle poverty.

Leaving home and social housing

Moving away from the family home to (relatively) independent living is an important part of the transition to adulthood. The majority of interviewees (27 of 34) had, by the time of the current study, left the parental home, although not always by choice. The sample's overall economic marginality and limited financial resources did *not* inhibit the ability of most to begin independent housing careers, but it certainly did have an impact on the options available to them and featured prominently in decisions not to leave.

Leaving home

A central factor in determining housing transitions was the relative poverty of the sample members. Few were able to afford the first steps on the private housing ladder. Those with most financial resources to call upon had the greatest room for manoeuvre. Two of the three 'owner occupiers' (Marje and Tara) were both part of dual-earning households and the third (Val) had a husband in a relatively secure, long-term job. Even some of those with reasonable incomes, such as Martin, possessed debts (Martin had debts of £17,000) that made house ownership unlikely for the time being at least. Although owner-occupation is higher among over 35-year-olds (Watt, 1996), regardless of age social renting is more likely to be undertaken by those on low incomes. The relative youth and the relative poverty of our sample made them less likely than the adult population in general to have sought private ownership.

Remaining in the parental home was a practical way of displacing and delaying the material costs of independent living. Seven people were still living with their parents. One of them, Alex, said "It's cheaper for me here". She paid a small amount to her parents from her low-paying care job, commenting: "Now you know why I stay!". Thus, living with parents disguised – and eased – personal poverty. The quality and stability of relationships with families of origin were also an important influence on decisions to leave or stay. Those older interviewees who had stayed living with their parents until their late twenties, such as Annie (27) and Max (28), described strong family bonds. The strength of family relations also underpinned decisions about where to move.

From their larger, national survey, Ford et al (2002a) suggest a typology of different sorts of youth housing career. Each type reflects the ability of young people to plan their moves and family resources, and the constraints that restrict housing options (such as finances and the nature of the local housing market). In our study, the majority of those who had left home appear to fall into what Ford et al describe as 'chaotic' and 'unplanned' housing pathways. It would be difficult to categorise any of our sample as fitting the other categories they describe, all of which involve greater degrees of planning, family support and moves in response to employment or educational opportunities. Chrissie, for example, dryly observed that "I'd like to go to Australia ... it's the furthest you can go before you start coming back". This is not to imply that *no* family support was lent to the moves our interviewees made, nor that some of those still living with parents might one day take more planned housing moves. The reasons why some remained with parents were exactly because they

wanted to bide their time until they were in a better position to establish independent living.

For our interviewees, the move to independent living was not necessarily a simple transition and some of their biographies exemplified very clearly what Ford and colleagues meant by a 'chaotic housing pathway' in which personal planning, family support, financial resources and choice were limited. Rapid movement through a succession of housing options tended to reflect a lack of personal control and planning in the lives of the young adults concerned. Unsurprisingly, then, it was a pattern most often reported by those in the 'criminal and/or drug-using' sub-sample, many of whom described biographies in which their actions were driven by heroin addiction rather than a more reasoned, strategic balancing of options. Here housing careers were complicated further by the likelihood of estrangement from family and siblings and by periods of penal incarceration. As noted in Chapter 2, a criminal record and a history of heroin use can seriously jeopardise access to social and privately rented housing.

This 'chaotic' pattern was not limited, however, to those with histories of dependent drug use and crime. When we first met her at the age of 23, Sarah, for instance, had changed residence 12 times. Her haphazard housing career – which began with her leaving the family home aged 15 after a row with her mother – reflected the mixed relationship that she had had with her parents and, later, the intense, often violent relationships with the fathers of her two children. When first interviewed, Sarah was living in a council house in East Kelby with her two children and her 14-year-old sister. She was reasonably happy with the area, liked the garden that the children could play in and planned to stay for a while. Our current study found her settled in the same house.

The relative abundance and availability of social housing in these neighbourhoods helped individuals like Sarah make eventual transitions to more settled, independent living (albeit in some cases after earlier, turbulent housing careers). At second interview, 25 of the sample members lived in some form of social housing (two others were in prison). For a few, the social housing they moved to brought other problems (see Martin, p 27) and some were yet to find secure or suitable accommodation (of whatever sort). Overall, though, most had made transitions to independent living and – despite their continued experience of poverty and economic marginality – their housing careers were beginning to show some stability.

The significance of place in housing careers: dreams of leaving

Interviewees' changing, varied and complicated perceptions of their home neighbourhoods emerged as important in understanding their previous housing careers and their current outlooks on their futures. Not only did assessments of home neighbourhoods vary between individuals, the same individuals could often readily describe both the difficulties and the advantages of living where they did.

In general terms, interviewees gave voice to the problems of living in Willowdene and East Kelby. The related problems of youth crime and drug use provided the major spur to dreams of leaving these places. But in no case was this sufficient to initiate a housing move, nor was it the sole reason referred to by those who hoped to move in the future. As in all these young adults' housing careers, a multiplicity of 'external' factors and personal issues came together in their housing ambitions.

At first interview, for example, a series of personal tragedies had energised Martin's *commitment* to his neighbourhood (see MacDonald and Marsh, 2001). When we met him again as part of this project, he was 23, had married his girl friend and left Primrose Vale behind. The key factor that had motivated his *abandonment* of the place to which he was previously so committed was the perinatal death of his first child. His wife became "very severely depressed", a situation worsened by the fact that at the time they were living in a rented flat in an East Kelby tower block that mainly housed noisy, sometimes disruptive, single young people:

> "… socially it was quite bad. There were a lot of young people. I'm trying to say young people 'cos I'm quite young myself, but there's quite a lot of young teenagers living there, probably 16, 17, 18, 19, cause a lot of noise and disturbance. In particular, on the night before we moved out, someone was actually bottled outside the flat door, which

was quite distressing obviously. It's just not an environment, really, that I want to be in."

So, although Martin referred to the potentially better employment factors to be found elsewhere and the problems of delinquency in his home neighbourhood, his actual move – to another council property in a north east town – was inspired by a desire to make a 'clean break' with profound personal loss, a move he described as going from a "nightmare" to a "dream".

The significance of place in housing careers: the costs of leaving

For those three people who had left Kelby (Carol-Anne, Martin and Danny), the formation of new partnerships was a significant factor in this process. This is shown in Carol-Anne's case, which also highlights the significance of place in the sample's housing careers and the complicated risks and opportunities involved in leaving Kelby. We give it considerable space because it also illustrates some of our more general findings and the way that we seek to theorise extended transitions.

A central conclusion of this and our previous studies is that the twists, turns and outcomes of the transitions of young adults can rarely be explained by reference to a single event or experiences confined to one aspect of such transitions (for example, the family or education, training and employment careers). A more holistic exploration of young adults' lives 'in the round' allows us to see how particular personal experiences are shaped by complicated, interlinked processes. In Carol-Anne's case we can also see how several processes and experiences associated with the transition to adulthood had paradoxical effects and contradictory meanings but, together, produced troubling psychological problems for her.

We interviewed Carol-Anne three times, first when she was 24 and working as an administrator for a training agency in East Kelby. By the age of 26 she had moved to Huddersfield to live with her new boyfriend whom she had met via an Internet chat-room. At this point we interviewed her for a second time. She described life away from East Kelby in glowing terms. She enjoyed her new job in Huddersfield; it allowed her to use her secretarial skills and the wage was "much better" than in her previous job (£4.50 rather than £3.50 per hour). In our most recent meeting with Carol-Anne she recalled, however, how the onset of her depression was rooted in these changed circumstances. She soon began to "hate" the work: "It was a small family business with a very high staff turnover and I was off with a tummy bug for a week so they sacked me". Although she had a doctor's note to prove her illness: "... I didn't feel at the time that I could do anything about it. I just didn't have the confidence. And I just felt it was all my fault ... that was sort of when my depression started really. Felt really bad about myself."

When pressed about this, she said:

"[The sacking was] not the cause, but a factor. There was all different things going on and it just built up. The house flooded ... and then there was the stuff with my brother and all that at the same time. It was like – *Help! Need Help!* [her emphasis]. I went to see the doctor and he gave me quite high anti-depressants and sleeping tablets and things.... It's like a tunnel and you just can't see no light at the end. Everything just seems dark and you don't think your life's going to get any better. That's how I felt at the time, for five or six months at least."

More significant than the flooding of their house, "all the different things" Carol-Anne referred to included the deaths of her uncle, aunt and cousin's baby daughter within a few months of each other. Carol-Anne valued strong family bonds and felt particularly close to her mother and father: "I was homesick for about a year and a half after I came here." She currently visits them in East Kelby at least once a month and telephones them everyday. A particular cause of concern – and factor in her depression – was the behaviour of her heroin-dependent, now estranged, brother:

"It got worse when I moved. [My parents] let him move back in [to the family home] and then he'd steal from them and then he'd go and then they'd let him back in. It was just a vicious circle ... mostly it was my brother [who caused me to be depressed], 'cos he just kept hurting my parents and seeing them hurt and me not being there ...

put a strain on me really because I kept thinking – 'Should I go back?'. I'd left them and they needed me."

This physical separation of Carol-Anne from her family in East Kelby – and the consequent limits to the emotional support that she could offer them, and vice versa – was, in her mind, the thing that caused her most unhappiness. Her brother had caused problems for the family before but now she felt too distant to offer much in the way of immediate help. Together with the quick succession of tragic deaths of members of her extended family, being unfairly dismissed from a job that she initially loved and the flooding of her new home, these events and experiences culminated in serious ill-health (she still received medication for depression). Paradoxically, the same process of leaving the parental home in Kelby, establishing a new home with her boyfriend and becoming a parent (Carol-Anne had a one-year-old son whom she spent most of her time looking after) had also brought her most happiness. For her, leaving East Kelby was both the "best and worst thing I've ever done ... if my family could move here, I'd have a perfect life really."

Leisure careers: making the most of 'staying in'

Our previous ESRC study identified 'leisure careers' as a useful concept through which to help understand long-term processes of youth transition (MacDonald and Marsh, 2002b). They can play an important role in shaping the social networks in which young adults operate which, in turn, play an important role in opening up and closing down the range of personal social identities and courses of action perceived as possible by young adults.

Constraints on leisure: money, families and jobs

Contrary to some accounts of British youth culture, the lifestyles of these young adults did not take shape in relation to the consumer cultures and 'supermarkets of style' now said to be important influences on youthful identities (Muggleton, 1997; Hollands, 2002). Rather, their accounts suggest a somewhat premature withdrawal from the sort of public leisure said to typify the youth phase (for example, at 26, Linda believed she was "too old for night-clubs now").

Overall, relative poverty seemed to be a main shaping factor in leisure careers. Where sample members did specify leisure activities they mostly listed those typical of the wider, adult population in Britain – for example, nights out to pubs, social clubs and nightclubs, or home-based activities such as drinking alcohol, watching TV, reading and playing computer games. Home-based leisure seems to have become an even more important part of the leisure lives of this group, particularly for the young mothers in the sample. Sally, a mother of six children, described the financial limitations on her social life. She visited a nightclub that provided free drinks. She could only afford to go, however, once a month and had to save up over the preceding weeks to be able to afford the £15 entrance fee. Chrissie – unemployed at most recent interview – explained "I just stay in and watch TV. I can't afford to go out."

A few with higher incomes seemed to be involved in more consumption-based leisure activities (such as visiting the cinema and eating in restaurants). The frequency with which our interviewees remarked that they were unable to afford a holiday was, however, particularly revealing of the financial constraints on leisure that the majority experienced. Even where interviewees did not have the costs of supporting children to consider, leisure activities were constrained by low income. Simon, for instance, was currently in a job but still could not go on holiday with his girlfriend and family because he was short of money. Linda explained why her family did not go on holiday:

"Well no, you go on holiday – you've gotta save big amounts of money. Holiday for me isn't the most important thing in the world. I'd rather decorate the house than go on holiday. I see the benefit of the house for the next year and a half. A holiday lasts us two weeks."

Poverty was not, however, the only limitation to leisure. The responsibilities and time constraints of parenthood and running a home also limited the time available for personal free time. For young mothers, then, leisure time was often spent with children, extended family and other friends (many of whom had children

themselves). Sarah explained: "I mean, you've got to plan everything around them [the children]. You just can't say 'I'm going out tonight'.... You can't just go to the shop, 'cos you've got to dress the kids to go the shop, you know? Just little things like that." Tara described organising a night out with her husband as like "planning a military operation".

One might expect those in the 'criminal and drug-using' sub-sample to have rather different leisure activities from those described by the others. This was true to some extent and certainly in retrospect. Early criminal and drug-using careers took shape as a form of alternative leisure. Committing crime and using drugs had been motivated, in part, by boredom: "The only reason why I've done it [heroin] in the past is 'cos I've been bored: nowt to do, no job, stuck in the house all day" (Richard). Several in the 'criminal and/or drug using' sub-sample attached importance to being 'fit' and working out, primarily in order to be able to 'look after themselves' (see Winlow, 2001). This was a leisure activity that also helped 'kill time' for those who were attempting to desist from heroin use, and it took the place of the daily routines of a drug–crime lifestyle. Max, for instance, did boxing and weight training and emphasised the importance of having things to do:

"If you ask me life's fucking ... it's shit. You need money and you need hobbies to fucking ... you know? Like, I get depressed, me, if I don't do summat. I get depressed. Like, if I was on the dole, I would of fucking ... probably ended up doin' myself in. I don't know how people survive on the dole, fuck that."

So, the leisure careers of our sample displayed the continuation of trends revealed in our earlier studies. For all sub-samples, leisure activities were primarily home-based and constrained by poverty. Further constraints for parents included the heavy demands of childcare and domestic work and, for some of those in employment, the unsociable and long hours of the jobs they did. The constraints they described are not unusual ones in that most families also need to balance the demands of childcare and employment, but the restrictions on leisure for this sample seemed particularly tight. The absence of holidays in the lives of interviewees was particularly revealing of this point.

Social networks: strong bonds but weak bridges

In tracing the development over time of individuals' leisure careers we can see as well the range and type of people with whom individuals choose to associate in their free time. Although an individual's social network is not restricted to those with whom they socialise (including, typically, family and work colleagues as well), these relationships of choice did much to shape how people saw themselves, their circumstances and their futures.

By examining social networks we can also begin to discuss the sort of 'social capital' to which our informants had access. By this we mean the advantages and disadvantages that can come from longer-term commitment to the social networks in which people operated (Bourdieu and Wacquant, 1992; Coleman, 1994; Forrest and Kearns, 2000; Putnam, 2000; Field, 2003). The research literature draws a distinction between 'bonding social capital' and 'bridging social capital'. 'Bonding social capital' refers to the strength of connections between individuals and their families and closest friends. 'Bridging social capital' refers to associations with people *beyond* one's immediate circle of family and friends. Many contributions to debates about social capital emphasise how social networks are advantageous in ways "that enable participants to act together more effectively to pursue shared objectives" (Putnam, 1996). Our study lends itself, however, to a more critical interpretation of the effects of social capital.

It was certainly the case that strong bonds across our informants' social networks helped in coping with life in poor communities. They offered emotional and financial support, childcare and access to job opportunities. They could also, however, exclude, marginalise, constrain and entrap people, and draw them into and maintain criminality and dependent drug use. The knowledge, views of the world and social and emotional resources that circulate in such networks can play an important role in influencing the steps taken in young adults' extended transitions. But social networks can also be restricting. Some of our evidence suggested that the trust and loyalties engendered through such ties could result in alternative opportunities being ignored. One mother, Linda,

for example, made the following comments about a local Sure Start scheme, despite never having visited it: "I can just imagine it'd be like a load of women whinging saying 'I've done this, I've done the other' and the kids playing about". This image was constructed via the anecdotal evidence of a close friend, the veracity of which Linda had not questioned.

While bonds with personal networks tended to be strong, few interviewees had maintained or established 'bridges' with wider networks of acquaintances. Since our earlier studies, the wider peer networks of teenage years had slimmed down and there was a general trend – across all sub-samples – toward socialising with, and receiving support from, family.

Those in the 'education, training and employment' sub-sample continued to have friends from work but, for some, the demands of their job – and in some cases new families – left little time for socialising. This meant that family members often were considered 'best friends'. Alex described her mother as her "best friend" and how they went on holidays together:

"... because I wouldn't have got on a plane if it wasn't for her [her mother]. It's just that she come in and told me it was booked and I have to go and I got on a plane. And I liked it so much, so we went back last year and we're going back this year."

For those in the 'family' sub-sample, friends who remained from the time of the first interview – and the new ones made since then – tended to be mothers themselves and live close by. Daily routines shaped by domestic and especially childcare responsibilities resulted in all the young mothers streamlining their lives down to what they considered most important and the benefits that accrue from these relations for their parenting career:

"Janine [Val's previous best friend] wanted me around there all the time.... She was wanting me to stay over 'cos she was on her own and I couldn't do it, with having me own family. We just drifted apart really. She hasn't bothered for a while now." (Val)

Our earlier studies showed that – for those involved in crime and drug use – social networks encouraged criminal activities that worked against wider community interests. Among the members of the 'criminal and drug-using' sub-sample in our current study, their involvement in social networks had very significantly changed. Earlier, neighbourhood-based social networks served as a form of social capital in accompanying, supporting and encouraging criminal and drug-using identities, offering protection and criminal opportunity, keeping going the momentum and excitement of lawlessness and drug use, providing skills and contacts and, crucially, offering a means of entering illicit local markets in drugs and stolen goods. As individuals in this sub-sample got older and custodial sentences more frequent, these neighbourhood networks extended into local prison populations. As individuals entered and were released from prison they could rely on a continuum of support through an exchange of similar populations between the two sites of neighbourhood and prison.

By second interview, however, interviewees in this sub-sample complained of the disruption and diffusion caused to social networks by regular incarceration and dependent drug use. Furthermore, these criminal and drug-using networks constrained the realisation of adult independence and the achievement of wider and different life goals (for example, of finding and sustaining partnerships or finding or staying in work) or immediate, contingent and often desperate goals (such as fighting addiction or saving a relationship). As individuals grew older and drug-criminal careers progressed, the earlier benefits that had accrued from social networks became liabilities. Micky was trying to desist from drugs with the support of his partner and her family. He talked about how dependent drug use led to increasing isolation as networks became restricted to other users only. He noted his struggle to escape from the people he had once considered friends:

"When you're on the drugs, no cunt wants to know ya. All they can remember is all the bad things about ya. Like when you're on the heroin, obviously anything you do is bad, 'cos that's all you fucking think about. You just think about the habit. You don't think about the people around you.... I haven't got none [best friends]. I'm trying to keep myself to myself 'cos, like, now you can find a best mate and he'll sit there and tell you he's clean and then two minutes

later, it'll be 'haway, let's go get fuckin' some gear [heroin]' and I'm like, 'I don't even wanna talk to you.'"

As a result, these social networks decreased in influence, as individuals reduced or relinquished previous associations, to be replaced by ones which were smaller in scope and more centred on partners and family members. Rebuilding bonds was, however, a difficult process. Continued relations with family were conditional on individual's demonstration of good behaviour and that they were 'staying clean'. Where for the other two sub-samples norms of reciprocity were open to negotiation, this condition, for this group, seemed non-negotiable. Amy had been off heroin since October 2002 when she was put on remand in a London prison for alleged drug offences. She was acquitted seven months later and returned to Kelby. She has become closer to her mother and sister, largely due to her drug desistance:

"They're [the family] really important now but I never realised when I was on the drugs 'cos you only think about your drugs. You don't think about nobody else.... Well, I've fucking tortured my family. I've tortured my Mam and Dad while they're in the house, you know? Putting all the windows in and smashing the cars and pinching ... nah, it's not summat you do."

Overall, then, the majority of informants had established very few new 'bridging ties' into networks beyond their close personal associations. Coping with the problems thrown up by their various careers and transitions meant, in fact, that their social networks had become smaller in scope, more focused on immediate family and friends and even more embedded in their immediate neighbourhoods. The geographic and social horizons of our interviewees tended, therefore, to be restricted to the place they were from. This process has important implications for longer-term possibilities in respect of their education, training and employment careers, which we spell out in Chapter 4.

'Critical moments': the unpredictable consequences of bereavement and ill-health

Our previous studies highlighted the important influence on youth transitions of what have been termed 'critical moments' (Thomson et al, 2002). Particular life events and experiences – such as parental separation, bereavement or episodes of ill-health – were found to have significant effects on the nature, direction and outcomes of an individual's transition to adulthood. Thus, while those we researched shared many social and economic experiences in common, some had quite different transitions, partly because of the influence of particular critical moments on their lives. This finding, which was confirmed again in this study, allows us to see how individual agency and decision making can operate within a context of shared poverty, economic marginality and – as we describe in Chapter 4 – shared, personal experiences of ill-health and loss.

The influence of personal agency was also illustrated in informants' experiences of bereavement. The personal consequences of and reactions to this sort of critical moment differed markedly between individuals and between individuals' separate instances of loss. Strikingly, over half reported the loss of a significant person in their lives (and this estimate does not include grandparents): that is, of parents, siblings, partners, children or friends. Typically these resulted from various chronic or acute illnesses, but accidents (for example, car crashes), drug overdoses and suicide also took their toll on members of the interviewees' families and social networks. The psycho-social effects of these bereavements were often significant in the later lives of the people to whom we talked, even though – and perhaps understandably – they were not quick to speak of these things.

We discussed Martin in Chapter 2 in respect of his 'successful' employment career and earlier in this chapter in respect of his housing career. His experience of ill-health and bereavement is what is of interest here. When we first interviewed him, Martin described how the suicide of his father and of a best friend had served to energise his commitment to his job ("I've worked a lot harder since it happened, for me own good ...") and to his neighbourhood. He established a grass roots youth group in order to improve conditions for local young people: "to fight back ... [and to] try and put myself right". His second interview came after his marriage to his girlfriend, his departure from Kelby and the perinatal death of his first child. Although his wife became "very severely depressed", Martin's own response to this tragedy was to sink himself into his job:

> "My way of mourning is basically to get to work and immerse myself in that, which is what I did when my Dad died. I had three days off and I was straight back to work. With Ben [his son] I had three weeks off but personally – if it was just me – I would have gone back straight away. It's just my way of dealing with things."

Martin's commitment to work, and the relative success he had achieved, is all the more interesting given the health problems he and his family have suffered. Shortly before the death of his child, Martin was diagnosed with Type 1 diabetes, after collapsing at work and being rushed to hospital: "I was lying in the hospital bed and burst into tears and thought 'why has another thing happened to me?'".

Martin's experience illustrates the way that individuals responded to bereavement, ill-health and other critical life events in unpredictable ways. There were many examples of this. Annie lost her brother when she was 11 years old. At the age of 27, she said "I think about it all the time, you know". Annie described how her other brother "went on drugs and stuff; he went inward on himself, as a result", whereas she was "quite level headed and kept everything together. I suppose I was 11 going on 21 ..." Other interviewees variously described 'going off the rails' and 'everything going wrong' following the death of a parent: the emotional shock associated with loss blew their previously straightforward teenage transitions off course, at least for a short period. In contrast, such experiences sometimes served to orient informants *away* from more risky activities. As noted in Chapter 2, for Micky the death of his mother was reported as the key, motivating factor behind his ambition to desist from a long-term career of dependent drug use: "It affected me in loads of ways. It's kept me off the drugs anyway. 'Cos I was a heroin addict. I was messing about with the heroin for the past four year and – since this has happened – I've straightened meself out."

The social and psychological consequences of a serious life event such as bereavement could play out over a long period and had implications for extended youth transitions that were not obvious at the time of the event itself. Max's stepfather died when Max was in his mid-teens. One longer-term consequence of this is that Max, now aged 28, feels firmly tied to Willowdene and to maintaining his local reputation as 'a handy lad' who can protect himself and his family (despite his emergent idea to move away to somewhere with greater personal opportunities):

"I don't really want to leave me Mam here, you know what I mean? If my Mam wasn't in this area I'd fuck off today. Like I say, she hasn't been burgled in 28 year but I'd put money on it that if I moved she would get burgled. That's why I make myself out to be hard. Like round here you've got to be a bastard to survive, you know what I mean? It's one of them things."

Max gave a further instance of the sort of dramatic life events that affected this group and the 'hard' response that some men, like him, tried to take towards them:

DS: You said you had two friends that had died?

Max: That's them two on that photo there, Steven and Dekker.

DS: So, what happened?

Max: Steven crashed in the car and hit a tree. I don't know if you heard about it on the news? The car burst into flames, upside down [This incident was well-known, particularly among our Willowdene interviewees. It was, however, not the only fatal car crash to affect those in our sample]. There were six of them in the car. I was the first one there 'cos it was right outside our house. Ginger's sister was there, Sharon. Steven. Steven died. Wayne. Wayne died. Sharon died. Ginger lost his legs. Smithy got burnt badly and another lad broke his arm. He hit the tree at 130mph, something like that.

DS: Were they just joy-riding?

Max: No, they were coming back from a club. They were on E [ecstasy].

DS: What about the other lad – Dekker was it?

Max: He died of alcohol poisoning. [later in the interview]

DS: What sort of impact do you think that these two deaths have had? I mean you obviously keep the photographs?

Max: Oh, it was fuckin' bad. It was just bad like. I'm glad that I'm working and that now, 'cos me head would be up me arse if I wasn't working like…. All the shit I've had in me life, it's my mates that have got me through it. There's a lot of people who say, "Have you seen a counsellor?". You know with the crash. I'm like, "No I don't fuckin' need counselling", you know what I mean?

While Martin and Max operated with quite different personal styles of masculinity, it is perhaps interesting to note that both men specified that working had been a strategy for staving off the psychological trauma that might otherwise have followed the loss of friends and parents (or, as Max more simply put it, "me head would be up me arse if I wasn't working.").

Given the multiple hardships and instances of loss suffered by our interviewees, it is unsurprising that many reported experiences of depression. As predicted by Brown and Harris (1978) and suggested by Martin's and Max's ways of coping with bereavement – women were more likely than men to describe to us the symptoms associated with often severe depressive episodes. Epidemiological surveys show depression to be concentrated among "women, the young and disadvantaged" (Hammen, 1997). That is not to suggest that the men in our study were immune to this form of psychological ill-health but that women appeared more likely to label their psychological experiences in this way and to seek medical assistance for it (Luck et al, 2000). Rather than make use of the available health and welfare services, some men – like Max – preferred to present a more resilient face to the world (and to us as researchers). Memorably – when we first met him four years ago – he told us that "only stone-faced fuckers" survived in Willowdene.

Summary and conclusions

Our study has been interested in the longer-term transitions of young people from neighbourhoods suffering social exclusion in extreme form. The earlier chapters of the report mapped processes of change and continuity and picked out common themes in the lives of our informants. This chapter summarises our main findings and tries to explain why their transitions into adulthood continued to be ones typified primarily by material poverty, economic marginality and social exclusion.

Continuity and change in extended transitions

The interviews with young adults presented something of a paradox. Many of them certainly *felt* that their lives had changed considerably since we last talked to them. Our earlier studies described youth transitions in this context as varied, precarious and multifaceted. Between the time of their first and most recent interview numerous events and experiences influenced individual biographies in ways that might not have been predicted. Buffeted by unanticipated critical moments – ill-health, parental separation or bereavement – these transitions were a complex set of twists and turns.

At case-by-case level this description still captures the nature of their transitions as they extended over time. As in earlier periods of their lives, the flux and fluidity of individual transitions engendered subjective feelings of personal change. Moreover, our most recent interviews revealed that the research participants *had*, in many cases, taken important steps in their lives in respect of housing and family careers. This is a significant finding given the lack of progress they

had made in respect of their education, training and employment careers and their continued experience of poverty. The formation of new partnerships, households and families, for a large proportion of our interviewees, constitutes real change and progress. The other, most noteworthy experience of change was had by a significant number of those people with extended drug-using and criminal careers. Compared with our first studies, several people now displayed serious commitment to desistance from their previous destructive lifestyles.

Thus, the study revealed not only a subjective sense of flux in personal lives but, for many in the sample, real changes in their housing, family, criminal and drug-using careers. These changes were played out in a situation where informants' general experiences of the economic aspects of transition remained constant. All but a few of the interviewees continued to express very conventional attitudes and attachment to work, even if several of those who were mothers still prioritised the care and upbringing of their children and had largely put concerted engagement with the labour market on hold until their children were older. Even some of those with the least promising work histories – from the 'criminal and drug-using' sub-sample – had nevertheless managed to access employment.

The work the interviewees did, however, was largely of the type they had encountered in their lives to date. Even that group who showed most commitment to and closest engagement with the labour market in our first studies had made little progress since. Theirs were still low-skilled, low-paid manual and service sector jobs at the bottom of the labour market. In this context, getting a job that paid £4.50, rather than £3.50, an hour was counted as a good outcome and potential jobs in call centres or as bus drivers were regarded as a step up. They did poor work, often for seemingly punitive employers who, according to these accounts, were as quick to fire as they were to hire willing workers.

The insecurity of jobs was a central feature of the economically marginal education, training and employment careers the interviewees described. The experience of training and employability schemes (of YT and NDYP in particular) that informants had amassed – prior to our first studies and since then – seemed to have had little positive impact on their chances of getting and remaining in employment. Dispiriting experiences of school did not predict later, wholesale rejection of formal learning. The majority had accessed further education and training courses since we last met them but remained poorly qualified. While the experience of these may have been enjoyable and they may have had useful social and personal functions (such as allowing young mothers time away from childcare and domestic work), these were mostly short, basic courses that, to date, had not helped them move to secure employment. Cyclical movement around jobs at the bottom of the labour market, unemployment and short-term or sometimes unfinished education and training courses remained the norm.

The description we give here, then, is virtually identical to the way we described these individuals' encounters with the labour market at earlier dates. That individuals were able to progress to a relatively more independent lifestyle and to begin families is commendable. That this was done in such inauspicious circumstances is further testament to their ability to get by in conditions of relative poverty. As described in Chapter 2, however, 'getting by' was also very much dependent on the practical, emotional and (albeit limited) financial support they received from their families (of origin and destination). The availability of social housing in these neighbourhoods, and the various welfare benefits that accrue, particularly to households with children, also made these sorts of transitions possible.

Thus, while individuals may have felt and experienced considerable change since we first met them, the economic aspects of the sample's transitions had remained largely unchanged. The local economy is crucial, we think, in shaping the

overall outcomes of their transitions, even if, at the individual level, people pointed to other aspects of change in their lives. As Bertaux and Thompson (1997) suggest, there is a tendency for individuals not to question the socioeconomic circumstances to which they have become accustomed, even when, by most standards, these would be regarded as highly restraining and unrewarding. Even where interviewees did not directly criticise the economic conditions under which they lived, these constraints emerged in passing comments. These included more profound statements about how progressing with a pregnancy was simply unaffordable to more mundane asides about limited leisure and the absence of holidays in their lives. Most in the sample were unable to afford products and activities that the majority in wider society feel are essential. In short, the constraints and opportunities afforded by the informants' economic situations overshadowed all other aspects of their transitions.

Social exclusion, poverty and social networks

We conclude, then, that social exclusion is a reasonably apt term to describe the situations our sample were in, if by social exclusion we mean the problems associated with relative poverty. One advantage of the concept of social exclusion is that it draws attention to the *multiplicity* of problems experienced by poor people. National league tables show the neighbourhoods in which our informants live to be ones in which the multiple problems of deprivation are most concentrated. Our study shows the lived experience of individuals who struggle to overcome these multiple hardships – of poverty, recurrent unemployment, personal and family ill-health, crime, problematic drug use and so on – as they make extended transitions to adulthood. The problems of social exclusion are interconnected, cumulative and a process. So, for our sample, the cumulative experience of earlier transitions compounded current situations and possibilities. Those whose earlier lives had been dominated by sporadic employment, childcare responsibilities or dependent drug use still contended with the legacy of these preoccupations at the time of the recent interviews.

Of course, the problems of social exclusion are not mutually exclusive and nor are the different dimensions that make up youth transitions. So, for instance, while some had more to tell than others about their attempts to progress housing, family or employment careers, virtually all were now more directly contending with these aspects of transition. Careers of crime and dependent drug use were the exception. There was no evidence of the later onset of criminal or drug-using careers within our sample. Typically, these commenced in teenage years and – as we have shown – many of those involved were now trying to bring these to a halt.

A further trend that was common to all sub-groups was the narrowing down and closing in of social networks, compared with the wider, peer networks of teenage years. Interviewees rarely operated outside their own, neighbourhood networks.

In the past, social mobility for Teesside residents has in part been facilitated by geographical mobility, yet this was rare for our interviewees. This is an area that has historically – and continues – to experience net out-migration (Webster et al, 2003). Those, usually younger, residents who *do* acquire higher skills and qualifications are prone to leave for more prosperous labour markets elsewhere.

Our informants' lack of access to wider networks makes individual or collective social mobility unlikely. Seldom did their networks of family and friends provide the sort of social capital that might assist in transcending the limiting socioeconomic conditions in which they lived. Indeed, they could be read as closing down opportunities (Strathdee, 2001). The best example of this can be found in the fact that such networks remained the key mechanism for jobsearch. Because those they used to help in finding jobs (that is, extended family networks and friends) were also typically confined to the same sectors of the labour market as them, our interviewees remained tied to insecure, poor work that offered little chance of personal progression.

De-industrialisation and the intergenerational experience of family disadvantage

We do not conclude, however, that the social exclusion experienced by our sample is in some way a direct product of their cultural practices, social networks and lifestyles. On the contrary, networks of family support proved indispensable in helping people keep their heads above water.

For us, the rapid and widespread de-industrialisation of a place that was, until relatively recently, one that 'worked', is central to any understanding of the contemporary, extended transitions of its young adults (Beynon et al, 1994; Byrne, 1999). What we see at the core of our interviewees' biographical accounts is their various, resourceful, resilient ways to live with the consequences of the collapse of the 'economic scaffolding' that previously enabled transitions to stable and secure working-class adult life (Salo, 2003).

In rooting our analysis in Teesside's industrial history we do not intend to romanticise communities that were characterised by hardship, the dangers of heavy industry, and rigid and oppressive sexual divisions of labour. Nevertheless Charlesworth's (2000, p 10) account of the comparatively recent dislocation of traditional working-class life provides a suitable epitaph for Kelby's decline:

"The loss of a way of living that was based upon hard work and industry, within which there was a sense of friendship and relation, of basic dignity and respect. Of something that one could live in. Of a once-present state now lost, in which individuals could plan a future, buy a house, marry and have children, live a life that, though constrained by the routines of work, offered some security and some circumscribed pleasures. However, the decline of traditional industry, and its replacement with jobs governed by new working practices have brought great vulnerability at work, through worry about the security of employment, its duration and the low pay most jobs offer."

The wider, global processes of economic change that have led to the de-industrialisation of places like Teesside have also given rise to a new 'information economy' sector, based predominantly on information technology, finance, retailing and some service sectors (Wilson, 1996; Castells, 2000a, 2000b). A key feature of the new 'information economy' is the premium placed on a high level of education and skills. Our informants seemed poorly positioned to take advantage of the graduate-level employment associated with expanding sectors of the economy. Our study touched on some of the difficulties that young adults from poor neighbourhoods faced when they attempted higher education. Questions remain about the availability of more rewarding, lucrative, graduate jobs for those who do manage to acquire higher level skills and qualifications but who remain living in de-industrialised poor towns like Kelby. Annie, the only person from our study who had gained an undergraduate degree, was contemplating seeking work in care homes or in the police service.

In short, Kelby is one of the places that has lost out in the shift from a predominantly industrial to a predominantly information economy. The fact that it is a town with the highest concentration of the most deprived wards in the country is testament to this (DETR, 2000). While the expansion of the service sector since the 1970s has, here as elsewhere, meant increasing rates of employment for women, often in part-time jobs, even this sector of employment contracted in Kelby during the 1990s. High rates of female joblessness persist in the neighbourhoods we studied.

These changes in the economic structure have been accompanied by the creation of increasingly polarised primary and secondary labour markets (Hutton, 1996). The former, compared with the latter, carry with them jobs that are better paid, higher skilled, more secure and of higher status. Despite the importance of the new 'information economy' at national and international levels, it is important not to over-predict the *disappearance* of low-skilled and low-paid jobs. These kinds of jobs continue to be found in Kelby – as our informants' work histories showed – but the *conditions* associated with them have worsened. Confined to jobs in the precarious secondary labour market and excluded from the new economy, 70% of Kelby's population live in deprived wards (Webster et al, 2003).

The concentration of poverty and multiple deprivation in Kelby has led some commentators to cite it as a place in which a culturally distinct, welfare underclass is likely to be found (Murray, 1994). Underclass theories implicate the poor as makers of their own poverty, particularly through the intergenerational transmission of allegedly delinquent, immoral and irresponsible 'cultures of poverty'. We found little evidence of this. Rather, virtually all the young adults in our study operated with highly conventional attitudes to family life and mainstream personal goals in respect of work that were remarkably durable, given the experiences they had. Some, as in our previous studies, turned the intergenerational inheritance of idleness on its head (unemployed Chrissie said "My father never had a job and I don't wanna be like him. I can get up at seven."). However, that is not to say there were no correspondences between their experiences and practices and those of their parents.

That they often came from families in which poverty, economic inactivity and 'benefit dependency' were also common reflects not some sort of inherited cultural disposition towards worklessness but the fact that these families of origin and destination shared the same structured conditions of disadvantage. Where they were still engaged in the labour market, most of their parents now also undertook insecure, marginal work (typically towards the end of working lives in which better skilled, working-class jobs had featured). Where they were not, this was often explained by disability and illness, not voluntary unemployment.

This latter point allows us to mention one further aspect of shared, intergenerational disadvantage. This concerns the problems of ill-health experienced by our interviewees. The sheer preponderance of physical and mental ill-health (particularly depression) in their lives and those of people close to them was striking, as was the extent of their experience of bereavement. Over half the interviewees reported the loss of a loved one after illness, suicide or accidents. Has Fate dealt our informants and their families a particularly unlucky hand or did we somehow recruit a skewed sample of the least healthy members of the local populace? We think neither is the case. Rather, representative statistics for the places we studied suggest that their experiences reflect socially structured health inequalities as they play out in poor neighbourhoods (Mitchell et al, 2000; Macintyre et al, 2002; Tees Valley Joint Strategy Unit, 2002). These experiences are typical of the class and place from which they come.

Learning from more successful transitions?

This overall summary has inevitably concentrated on the general findings of our study. A few individuals displayed more successful outcomes, particularly in respect of their education, training and employment careers. What can we learn from such cases that might help others in these contexts to make progress in their extended transitions?

Marje had liked school, been a good pupil and avoided the "bad ones". She left with some lower grade GCSEs at 16 and was then continuously employed in a succession of hairdressing jobs. She had met her partner at age 15 and married at 23. By second interview, aged 26, she was employed as a youth worker for a small voluntary sector agency, working with disadvantaged young people. By this time she had given birth to her daughter, was buying a house with her husband (also employed full-time), lived near and continued to have close ties with her family of origin who provided informal, unpaid childcare. She felt ambiguous about staying in a run-down area while realising that moving might be expensive.

At this point of our discussion we draw attention to a significant factor that seems to have been important in shaping Marje's relative success: the nature of her employer. Her earlier jobs in hairdressing did not 'predict' Marje's later employment as a youth worker. This came about because Marje had – while employed as a hairdresser – been involved in delivering YT at a local Further Education (FE) college. She enjoyed this work and noticed an advertisement for a full-time job working with disadvantaged school-leavers. She applied and was taken on by her current employer because, she feels, in part they were keen to offer the post to someone who came from a not too dissimilar background from their 'clients'. The supportive, beneficent ethos of this agency towards socially excluded young people extended to her too and was further demonstrated by the fact that they funded her part-time, distance learning degree (in youth work) and allowed her two study days a week.

At the time of her most recent interview Marje was the best paid member of the sample, enjoyed her job and had had continuous employment since leaving school. She was married and owned her own home. The fact that her qualifications at 16 were not markedly better than those of the majority supports our finding, from this and earlier studies, that formal qualifications at 16 in themselves do not predict later outcomes, at least not among the relatively poorly qualified. Marje's comparatively positive attitude to school may, though, be important for later re-engagement with education and training. Her association with peer networks who generally shared an instrumental, rather than disaffected, orientation to school helped maintain school engagement and disinclined her towards teenage truancy and delinquency.

Marje's post-school apprenticeship seemed a more effective route to a 'proper job' than the sorts of training schemes most others in the sample had entered. Entering work that she enjoyed and to which she was committed was part of the reason why she had continuous employment when most had more sporadic engagement with jobs. She avoided crime and drug use. Her parents were supportive and her husband was in full-time employment. Acceptable, informal childcare support was available so she was able to remain in her job after the birth of her daughter. Critically, she now worked for a benign, particularly supportive employer who encouraged her to undertake a part-time degree and allowed her two days a week study time.

Evoking Marje's atypical, 'successful' case allows us to cast light on the more typical, 'unsuccessful' cases of the majority. A *combination* of the various, positive biographical experiences and circumstances that we described earlier seemed crucial in ensuring Marje's relative success. When this sort of balance of beneficial factors 'comes together' across the range of an individual's careers, then progress towards satisfactory outcomes becomes more likely. Now consider the typical range and combination of factors and experiences found among and influencing the sample in general. They included dispiriting school experiences; a collapsed, low-waged, local labour market; attached poor quality training opportunities; casualised, insecure jobs with few employment rights; predominantly social housing (some of which brought problems of its own); limited or fragile childcare support; often close and supportive but sometimes precarious and traumatic family relationships; intergenerational poverty; personal and family ill-health; the prevalence of dependent drug use and crime in their home neighbourhoods; and a depressing physical and social environment.

In short, for most interviewees there was little evidence of the sort of 'positive' factors present in Marje's biography that might facilitate their overcoming the numerous, interconnected barriers and hurdles they faced over time. Moreover, it is difficult to envisage how – through personal effort alone – these individuals might escape the conditions in which they live. Despite their harbouring of very conventional attitudes and desires for the future, it seems that 'poverty jobs' will be, at best, the final destination of our sample and economic marginality a long-term future. We consider in the final chapter of the report what, if any, policy interventions might change this prediction.

5

Implications for policy

The causes and effects of social exclusion

We are hesitant about listing policy suggestions in respect of the findings that we have summarised earlier. We could, if space allowed, identify numerous ways that current interventions might be improved in respect of the problems associated with poor work, ineffective training, drug treatment, educational dis-engagement, childcare, leisure provision, the criminal justice system and so on that we have described. Because we took a rounded view of the lived experiences of individuals and explored the many dimensions of their transitions to adulthood, any list made would involve many different and complex policy interventions or reforms that implicate and impact upon socially excluded young adults. Such a list, if implemented, might help some of the individuals we talked to deal with some of the particular problems that they encountered.

We are resistant to sketching out such a list of policy remedies and adjustments of this sort because at best it will deal only with the effects of poverty, economic marginality and social exclusion, and offer little that might change the underlying causes and conditions that create them. For example, defining ways in which to improve drugs education, to better control drug supply and markets and to revise the treatment of addicts are all laudable exercises but none tackles the social and economic conditions which give 'poverty drugs' their appeal (MacDonald and Marsh, 2002a; Webster and Robson, 2002). Despite various initiatives of these sorts over the past 10 years, Teesside continues to have some of the deepest problems of drug-related crime and youthful addiction in the country (Home

Office, 2003). Similarly, a whole raft of anti-poverty initiatives in the past and recently – such as Sure Start, Tax Credits and New Deal – have been implemented in Kelby; yet it remains the poorest district in England. The failure of such initiatives beyond the temporary respite they may bring to some individuals is unlikely to be only a problem of presentation or targeting.

Instead we offer a concluding discussion that asks some more strategic, higher level questions about current policy agendas and resultant interventions towards tackling poverty, social inclusion and exclusion. While we do not have the space to specify every point of connection, we should add that this detailed, close-up ethnography of the lived experience of extended transitions for socially excluded young adults leads us to strongly endorse the general, over-arching proposals for the redirection of government policy towards poor people and places presented in the JRF's recent overview *Tackling disadvantage: A 20-year enterprise* (Darton et al, 2003).

Principles and practice for tackling social exclusion

According to Darton et al (2003) a broad-based strategy for tackling poverty needs to be underpinned by certain principles. These principles would seem to currently shape government policy. They are that poorer households and communities benefit from the market economy; an adequate basic income is needed for everyone; also access to necessary resources such as housing and care; and that, in the implementation of policies, there is no discrimination. Again although laudable, our study suggests that such principles are not being delivered in practice and the current mechanisms for their delivery are not having the desired effect.

For example, New Deal will reflect the local labour market conditions and context in which it operates. In our study, poor and casualised local labour market opportunities meant that individuals were placed in New Deal options that they did not want, were short-lived, were of poor quality and provided little long-term benefit in terms of future occupation. They did not enhance educational opportunities for the less well qualified (Furlong et al, 2003), and led to low-waged, unrewarding and insecure employment.

Those sample members experiencing family poverty and in receipt of Working Tax Credit and Child Tax Credit thought them important and welcomed them in alleviating low income. Our evidence suggested, however, that one-parent families – those most in need – benefited least from these credits. Young mothers who were unable to work because they prioritised childcare over employment, or experienced difficulties with childcare arrangements, did not benefit. Those in employment and receiving tax credits were trapped in poor work, and those without children were not eligible. Child Tax Credit would seem to offer a better mechanism for reducing poverty among young mothers because it is paid to all primary carers regardless of type of family or if they are, or are not, in paid employment. Tax credits and other benefits, however, engender a complicated trade-off between gaining and losing income through means testing, and between not working and poor work. Those sample members using services delivering support to parents with young children such as Sure Start were very positive about them. Others either didn't know about these services or felt them to be inflexible in providing the childcare support they needed. Initiatives geared to encouraging lone parents to work need to take account of local labour market conditions – the quality and availability of work – and personal circumstance and life events – for example, the need for flexible childcare, current health problems and social misfortune that can influence or delay the ability to work.

Anti-poverty policies and initiatives that ignore the underlying problem of poor work will not lift people out of poverty. Among ex-offenders and dependent drug users such policies and initiatives can become almost irrelevant as they face discrimination in areas such as housing and employment at every turn.

Extended, holistic and 'joined-up' policy or 'employability'?

As in our earlier studies we found that the problems associated with youth transitions do not conclude at neat, age-specific points and, therefore, age-related policies (such as the Connexions Service and NDYP) do not 'fit' harmoniously with the realities of the extended transitions that our sample members have undertaken. While policies to attack poverty need to be widely focused, they also need to be longer-term and sustained throughout transitions to adulthood (Catan, 2003). The joining up of different areas of policy such as family, housing, drug treatment policy and labour market policy towards the 'joined-up' problems of social exclusion (Coles, 2000) remains important. However, this wider, longer-term agenda has been displaced by a narrower, shorter-term 'employability agenda'.

In conditions of poor work and a precarious local labour market we question the appropriateness of the 'employability agenda' – moving people from welfare to work – that permeates current government policy towards socially excluded young adults living in poor neighbourhoods. We are not saying that employment is unimportant in alleviating poverty and social exclusion; on the contrary, paid employment is important as a route out of disadvantage. Most importantly, it can provide the income that lifts people out of poverty and its associated problems. This has not happened, however, for our sample. Most of the many jobs they and their partners had occupied have been insecure, low-paid, unskilled and lacking in prospects. They operated in a local labour market typified by pervasive under-employment and unemployment. Tax credits and other benefits received simply boost the low pay from these jobs to something nearer a decent living level. These are the sorts of unattractive low-level jobs that will always be present in local labour markets whether or not, at national level, we witness the arrival of the high-tech, high-skill information economy that some foresee. Under current arrangements, there is every possibility that this sort of poor work will continue to form the basis of economic life for our sample, and their children in future years.

Our diagnosis of why their extended transitions into adulthood are continuing to be hindered by the conditions of social exclusion closely implicates de-industrialisation and the decline of a once buoyant heavy industrial manufacturing sector within the local economy. This structural factor has caused a decline in the number of 'decent' jobs available locally and this and the resultant poverty is a cardinal reason for the disadvantaged positions that our sample members find themselves in as they have moved through the life-course. Problems of poor demand for labour and a paucity of realistic opportunity, training and support in respect of 'decent' work characterise the 'conditions of choice' for our sample. Becoming a young parent, having a criminal record or being drug dependent clearly make 'successful' employment transitions even more difficult, but economic marginality was a condition shared by our *whole* sample. These are conditions of the place, not (just) the individuals we studied.

Area regeneration, social integration and the redistribution of wealth

While our findings, analysis and conclusions recognise place as important in understanding the problems of extended transitions and social exclusion, we raise further questions about the government's continuing commitment to privileging area as the conduit for social inclusion policies. Since the 1980s, Teesside has been the subject of repeated rounds of government programmes for economic and social regeneration (for example, City Challenge, the Single Regeneration Budget, New Deal for Communities), but they have been unable to *solve* the persistent, long-term and various problems of de-industrialisation, structural unemployment and entrenched poverty. Area-based programmes do have a *potential* to help move people onto more progressive, upward paths if employment preparation and training connects with real employment (with greater security, opportunities for further training and promotion and pay) in sectors where there are

labour shortages (Simpson and Cieslik, 2000; Lupton, 2003). For us, the key shortcoming of area-based policies to counter social exclusion is that they cannot address the national and international trends that make particular places economically marginal and create some groups as socially excluded (Byrne, 1999; Lupton, 2003).

This brings us to our main policy conclusion. Youth policies like Connexions and NDYP propose remedies that imply the problem of exclusion lies in the deficits of the target population who, without the necessary or right sorts of knowledge and skills, are unable to take advantages of the opportunities said to exist. Therefore policies for young adults in poor neighbourhoods are usually geared towards employability and training schemes, help with jobsearch, interview and personal skills. This ignores, however, the availability and quality of existing employment opportunities in places like Teesside. The problem is framed in terms of the supply of labour being poor quality, not the poor quality of the demand for labour. Yet, *both* the supply *and* demand of labour decide the development and nature of employment opportunities. Historically the availability and quality of existing employment opportunities in Teesside has actually declined to the extent that, in comparison with the occupational positions of their parents and grandparents, young adults in our study have undergone marked intra-class, intergenerational downward mobility (Toynbee, 2003). In this context, the narrow supply side labour market initiatives described earlier – New Deal, Sure Start, Working Tax Credit, Child Tax Credit and so on – may in effect collude with or even reward, rather than challenge, the prevalence of poor work in places like Teesside. Getting people into poor work hardly addresses the multiple hardships and disadvantages of growing up in poor neighbourhoods.

Policy conclusions

The British 'welfare to work' agenda was initially inspired by the American system of 'Workfare', but even Workfare's main advocate suggested that in the British context:

"Workfare does assume that jobs are available to recipients required to work.... Some regions are historically depressed, particularly in the north, and it might be necessary to create some jobs there if all the dependent are to work." (Mead, 1997, p 127)

Of course, such an admission does not address the *quality* of the jobs so created. The availability of low-paid work does not resolve poverty and exclusion, as Polly Toynbee suggests:

"What if work, hard demanding, important work, does not liberate people from poverty at all? 'Work for those who can, welfare for those who can't', 'A hand up, not a hand out', 'Work is the best welfare' – these were Labour's mantras and they chimed with the spirit of the times. But what if they disguise the awkward fact that that work pays so little that those on the minimum wage are still excluded, marginalised, locked out?" (Toynbee, 2003, p 3)

Current policy emphasises supposed deficits in employability and skills among marginalised adults. This is to be rectified by training, advice, incentives and childcare support. However, this marginal redistribution of income and opportunity will not lift people out of poverty, unless they have access to good quality training and rewarding and secure employment. Poor training and poor employment opportunities tend to be synonymous. Income from decent rather than poor work, for those able to work, is the best way of lifting people out of poverty. Although the minimum wage raises the income threshold of poor work for some, it does not resolve how people might progress beyond this 'minimum'. Those who are unable, or 'choose' to delay work, because of childcare responsibilities and/or the disincentives of poor work, need more generous Income Support to lift them out of poverty traps. This might in the short term have the effect of deterring individuals from seeking poor work, but it may also have the beneficial longer-term effect of deterring poor offers of work. A more comprehensive and generous redistribution of resources and opportunities, such as the creation of available and accessible good quality training, flexible childcare and decent jobs, might allay the longer-term social exclusion and economic marginality experienced by the individuals featured in this report. We suggest that the current government's much-vaunted 'joined-up' policy towards reducing poverty and social exclusion, to be effective, needs to rediscover demand-side labour market reform by creating more secure, better quality, decent jobs in places like Teesside.

References

Bertaux, D. and Thompson, P. (1997) *Pathways to social class: A qualitative approach to social mobility*, Oxford: Clarendon.

Beynon, H., Hudson, R. and Sadler, D. (1994) *A place called Teesside*, Edinburgh: Edinburgh University Press.

Bourdieu, P. and Wacquant, L. (1992) *An invitation to reflexive sociology*, Chicago, IL: University of Chicago Press.

Bronfenbrenner, U. (1979) *The ecology of human development: Experiments by nature and design*, Cambridge, MA: Harvard University Press.

Brown, G. and Harris, T. (1978) *The social origins of depression*, London: Tavistock.

Brown, P. and Scase, R. (eds) (1991) *Poor work: Disadvantage and the division of labour*, Milton Keynes: Open University Press.

Byrne, D. (1999) *Social exclusion*, Milton Keynes: Open University Press.

Castells, M. (2000a) *The rise of the network society* (2nd edn), Oxford: Blackwell.

Castells, M. (2000b) *End of millennium* (2nd edn), Oxford: Blackwell.

Catan, L. (2003) 'Youth citizenship and social change: background to the youth research programme' at www.tsa.uk.com/YCSC/backg.html

Charlesworth, S. (2000) *A phenomenology of working class experience*, Cambridge: Cambridge University Press.

Coleman, J. (1994) *Foundations of social theory*, Cambridge, MA: Belknap Press.

Coles, B. (2000) *Joined up youth research, policy and practice: An agenda for change?*, Leicester: Youth Work Press.

Craine, S. (1997) 'The Black Magic Roundabout: cyclical transitions, social exclusion and alternative careers', in R. MacDonald (ed) *Youth, the 'underclass' and social exclusion*, London: Routledge.

Darton, D., Hirsch, D. and Strelitz, J. (2003) *Tackling disadvantage: A 20-year enterprise*, York: Joseph Rowntree Foundation.

Daycare Trust (2003) *Facing the childcare challenge*, Briefing Paper, London: Daycare Trust.

DETR (Department of the Environment, Transport and the Regions) (2000) *Index of multiple deprivation 2000*, London: DETR.

Dolton, P., Dyson, A., Meagher, N. and Robson, E. (2002) *ROUTES: Youth transitions in the north east of England*, ESRC Youth, citizenship and social change programme, Research Briefing, no 3.

DWP (Department for Work and Pensions) (2003) 'Households below average incomes, 2001/2002', at www.dwp.gov.uk/asd/hbai/hbai2002/contents.asp

ESRC (Economic and Social Research Council) (2002) *Hard times: Youth, disadvantage and transitions to adulthood*, Youth, citizenship and social change programme, Dissemination Report, no 2, Autumn.

ESRC (2003) *Mixed blessings?: The role of the family in young people's transitions to adulthood*, Youth, citizenship and social change programme, Dissemination Report, no 3, Spring.

Field, J. (2003) *Social capital*, London: Routledge.

Ford, J.R., Rugg, J. and Burrows, R.J. (2002a) 'Conceptualising the contemporary role of housing in the transition to adult life in England', *Urban Studies*, vol 39, no 13, pp 2455-67.

Ford, J.R., Burrows, R.J. and Rugg, J. (2002b) *Young people, housing and the transition to adult life*, ESRC Youth, citizenship and social change programme, Research Briefing, no 1, Autumn.

Forrest, R. and Kearns, A. (2000) 'Social cohesion, social capital and the neighbourhood', Paper presented to ESRC Cities Programme Neighbourhoods Colloquium, Liverpool.

Furlong, A. (1992) *Growing up in a classless society? School to work transitions*, Edinburgh: Edinburgh University Press.

Furlong, A. and Cartmel, C. (1997) *Young people and social change*, Milton Keynes: Open University Press.

Furlong, A., Cartmel, F., Biggart, A., Sweeting, H. and West, P. (2003) *Youth transitions: Patterns of vulnerability and processes of social inclusion*, Edinburgh: Scottish Executive.

Hammen, C. (1997) *Depression*, East Sussex: Psychology Press.

Hills, J., Le Grand, J. and Piachaud, D. (2002) *Understanding social exclusion*, Oxford: Oxford University Press.

Hollands, R. (2002) 'Divisions in the dark', *Journal of Youth Studies*, vol 5, no 2, pp 25-39.

Home Office (2003) at www.drugs.gov.uk/News/PressReleases/1043148808/news_full_view

Hutton, W. (1996) *The state we're in*, London: Vintage.

Johnston, L., MacDonald, R., Mason, P., Ridley, L. and Webster, C. (2000) *Snakes and ladders: Young people, transitions and social exclusion*, Bristol/York: The Policy Press/Joseph Rowntree Foundation.

Jones, G. (2002) *The youth divide: Diverging paths to adulthood*, Joseph Rowntree Foundation Young People Programme, York: York Publishing Services.

Jones Finer, C. and Nellis, M. (eds) (1998) *Crime and social exclusion*, Oxford: Blackwell.

Laub, J. and Sampson, R. (2003) *Shared beginnings, divergent lives: Delinquent boys to aged 70*, Cambridge, MA: Harvard University Press.

Levitas, R. (1998) *The inclusive society?: Social exclusion and New Labour*, Basingstoke: Macmillan.

Loveridge, R. and Mok, A.L. (1979) *Theories of labour market segmentation: A critique*, Den Haag: Nijhoff.

Luck, M., Williamson, T. and Banford, M. (2000) *Men's health*, Oxford: Blackwell.

Lupton, R. (2003) 'Neighbourhood effects': Can we measure them and does it matter?, CASEPaper 73, London: London School of Economics and Political Science.

MacDonald, R. and Marsh, J. (2001) 'Disconnected youth?', *Journal of Youth Studies*, vol 4, no 4, pp 373-91.

MacDonald, R. and Marsh, J. (2002a) 'Crossing the Rubicon: youth transitions, poverty drugs and social exclusion', *International Journal of Drug Policy*, no 13, pp 27-38.

MacDonald, R. and Marsh, J. (2002b) 'Street corner society: young people, social exclusion and leisure careers', ESRC Youth Citizenship and Social Change Conference, Brighton.

MacDonald, R. and Marsh, J. (2005: forthcoming) *Disconnected youth? Growing up in poor Britain*, Basingstoke: Palgrave.

MacDonald, R., Mason, P., Shildrick, T., Webster, C., Johnson, L. and Ridley, L. (2001) 'Snakes and ladders: in defence of studies of transitions', *Sociological Research Online*, vol 5, no 4.

Macintyre, S., MacIver, S. and Sooman, A. (2002) 'Area, class and health: should we be concentrating on places or people?', in S. Nettleton and U. Gustaffson (eds) *The sociology of health and illness reader*, Cambridge: Polity Press.

Mead, L. (1997) *From welfare to work: Lessons from America*, London: Institute of Economic Affairs.

Mitchell R., Shaw, M. and Dorling, D. (2000) *Inequalities in life and death: What if Britain were more equal?*, Bristol/York: Joseph Rowntree Foundation/The Policy Press.

Muggleton, D. (1997) 'The post-subculturalist', in S. Redhead with D. Wynne and J. O'Connor (eds) *The clubcultures reader: Readings in popular cultural studies*, Oxford: Blackwell.

Murray, C. (1990) *The emerging British underclass*, London: Institute of Economic Affairs.

Murray, C. (1994) *Underclass: The crisis deepens*, London: Institute of Economic Affairs.

New Policy Institute (2003) *Monitoring poverty and social exclusion 2003*, York: Joseph Rowntree Foundation/York Publishing Services.

Parker, H., Bakx, K. and Newcombe, R. (eds) (1988) *Living with heroin: The impact of a drugs 'epidemic' on an English community*, Milton Keynes: Open University Press.

Parker, H., Aldridge, J. and Eddington, R. (2001) *UK drugs unlimited: New research and policy lessons on illicit drug use*, Basingstoke: Palgrave.

Parker, H., Bury, C. and Eggington, R. (1998) *New heroin outbreaks among young people in England and Wales*, Police Research Group, Paper 92, London: Home Office.

Putnam, R.D. (1996) 'Who killed civic America?', *Prospect*, vol 7, no 24, pp 66-72.

Putnam, R.D. (2000) *Bowling alone: The collapse and revival of American community*, New York, NY: Simon and Schuster.

Reilly, M. and Eynon, C. (2003) *Miserable measures: The range and severity of measures of deprivation for the County Durham and Tees Valley area*, Public Health Intelligence Service: County Durham and Tees Valley Public Health Network.

Salo, E. (2003) 'Negotiating gender and personhood in the new South Africa', *European Journal of Cultural Studies*, vol 6, no 3, pp 345-565.

Sampson, R.J. and Laub, J.H. (1993) *Crime in the making: Pathways and turning points through life*, London: Harvard University Press.

Simpson, D. and Cieslik, M. (2000) 'Expanding study support nationally: implications from an evaluation of the East Middlesbrough Education Action Zone's Programme', *Educational Studies*, vol 26, no 4.

Society Guardian (2003) 'Far from certain', 8 October.

Strathdee, R. (2001) 'Change in social capital and "risk" in school to work transitions', *Work, Employment and Society*, vol 15, no 2, pp 1-16.

Tees Valley Joint Strategy Unit (2003) *Ward statistics*, at www.teesvalley-jsu.gov.uk/

Thomson, R., Bell, R., Holland, J., Henderson, S., McGrellis, S. and Sharpe, S. (2002) 'Critical moments: choice, chance and opportunity in young people's narratives of transition', *Sociology*, vol 36, no 2, pp 335-54.

Toynbee, P. (2003) *Hard work: Life in low-pay Britain*, London: Bloomsbury.

Watt, P. (1996) 'Social stratification and housing', *Sociology*, vol 30, no 3, pp 533-50.

Webster, C. and Robson, G. (2002) *Needs assessment of young substance misusers and drug services in Stockton*, Stockton: Stockton Drug Action Team and Drug Prevention Advisory Service.

Webster, C., Blackman, T., Sapsford, R. and Neil, B. (2003) *Social and community cohesion in Middlesbrough: A report to Middlesbrough Council*, Middlesbrough: Middlesbrough Borough Council.

Wilson, W.J. (1996) *When work disappears: The world of the new urban poor*, New York, NY: Alfred Knopf.

Winlow, S. (2001) *Badfellas: Crime, tradition and new masculinities*, Oxford: Berg.

Appendix:
Cross-sectional profile
of the achieved sample

Pseudonym	Sub-sample	Details at 1999 interview: age; employment status; qualifications (education and training); housing; drug use; criminal activity	Details at 2003 interview: age; employment status; qualifications (education and training); housing; drug use; criminal activity
'Broderick'	Crim/DU	Age 18; HMP; two GCSEs; limited drug use; criminal activity.	Age 22; F/T employed; no further qualifications; living with partner and child; claims no current criminal activity.
'Harry'	Crim/DU	Age 19; HMP; no qualifications; criminal activity.	Age 23; F/T employed; parents' home; no drug use; claims no current criminal activity.
'Max'	Crim/DU	Age 24; unemployed; no qualifications; mother's home; cannabis use; criminal activity.	Age 28; F/T employed; no further qualifications; lives alone; no drug use; claims no current criminal activity.
'Micky'	Crim/DU	Age 21; HMP; no qualifications; heroin dependent; criminal activity.	Age 25; unemployed; no further qualifications; bail address; claims no current heroin use or criminal activity.
'Richard'	Crim/DU	Age 20; HMP; low GCSEs; YT; heroin dependent; criminal activity.	Age 23; unemployed; City & Guilds; lives with partner and her two children; methadone treatment; claims no current criminal activity.
'Danny'	Crim/DU	Age 21; HMP; no GCSEs; heroin dependent; criminal activity.	Age 24; unemployed but 'fiddle' jobs; lives with partner, stepchild and their daughter; drug treatment programme; claims no current criminal activity.
'Tim'	Crim/DU	Age 20; unemployed; no GCSEs; NVQ levels 1 & 2; mother's home; heroin dependent; criminal activity.	Age 24; New Deal; lives with partner and stepdaughter; methadone programme; claims no current criminal activity.
'John'	Crim/DU	Age 28; unemployed; no qualifications; lives alone; heroin dependent; some criminal activity.	Age 34; unemployed; no further qualifications; lives alone; one child but limited contact; no partner; methadone programme; criminal activity.
'Stuart'	Crim/DU	Age 28; unemployed but 'fiddle' jobs; City & Guilds; no GCSEs; lives with partner, their child and stepson; claims no criminal activity.	Age 34; unemployed but 'fiddle' work; no further qualifications; lives alone; methadone treatment; some criminal activity.

Pseudonym	Sub-sample	Details at 1999 interview: age; employment status; qualifications (education and training); housing; drug use; criminal activity	Details at 2003 interview: age; employment status; qualifications (education and training); housing; drug use; criminal activity
'Amy'	Crim/DU	Age 24; unemployed; no qualifications; homeless hostel; heroin/crack use; criminal activity.	Age 28; unemployed; lives with friend; no heroin use and no drug treatment; new partner; claims no current criminal activity.
'Jason'	Crim/DU	Age 21; HMP; no qualifications; heroin/crack dependent; criminal activity.	Age 25; HMP; no qualifications; continued drug use; some drug dealing; no partner; no children.
'Dougie'	Crim/DU	Age 21; HMP; no GCSEs; partner; one child; heroin dependent; criminal activity.	Age 25; HMP; NVQ levels 1, 2 & 3; one child in care of his mother; no treatment while in HMP; claims to be using and dealing drugs in HMP.
'Sarah'	FAM	Age 23; low grade GCSEs; NVQ level 2; F/T university student; lives with her two children.	Age 27; New Deal; leaves degree course after 2nd year; lives with two children and partner; recreational drug use; no crime.
'Sophie'	FAM	Age 19; unemployed; low GCSEs; YT; lives with child; no crime.	Age 23; unemployed; no further qualifications; lives with child; no drug use; no crime.
'Alison'	FAM	Age 20; unemployed; GCSEs; YT but no qualifications; lives with partner and their two children; no criminal activity.	Age 24; unemployed; no further qualifications; lives with partner and two children; no drug use; no crime.
'Linda'	FAM	Age 23; unemployed; GCSEs (B, C & E grades); YT (NVQ levels 1 & 2); lives with partner and their child; no drug use; no crime.	Age 26; unemployed; no further qualifications; no drug use; no crime.
'Tara'	FAM	Age 22; F/T employed; GCSEs and 2 A levels, NVQ level 2; lives with partner and two children; no drug use; no crime.	Age 25; F/T employed (hairdresser); no further qualifications; lives with partner and three children; no drug use; no crime.
'Nicky'	FAM	Age 22; unemployed; low GCSEs; NVQ levels 1 & 2; lives with child; no drug use; no crime.	Age 25; unemployed; no further qualifications, education or training; lives with partner and two children; no drug use; no crime.
'Sally'	FAM	Age 24; unemployed; GCSEs (A, B & C passes); YT but no other qualifications; lives with four children and partner; no drug use; no crime.	Age 27; unemployed but P/T college student; lives with six children; no drug use; no crime.
'Val'	FAM	Age 18; unemployed; GCSEs (grades unknown); YT but no qualifications; lives with partner and their child; no drug use; no crime.	Age 22; unemployed; no further qualifications, education or training; lives with partner and two children; no drug use; no crime.
'Alice'	FAM	Age 18; unemployed; GCSEs (low grades); lives with partner and two children; no drug use; no crime.	Age 22; unemployed; no further qualifications; lives with partner and three children; no drug use; no crime.
'Mary'	FAM	Age 19; unemployed; GCSEs (grades unknown); lives with child; no drug use; no crime.	Age 23; P/T employed; no further qualifications, education or training; lives with child; no drugs; no crime.

Pseudonym	Sub-sample	Details at 1999 interview: age; employment status; qualifications (education and training); housing; drug use; criminal activity	Details at 2003 interview: age; employment status; qualifications (education and training); housing; drug use; criminal activity
'Charlotte'	FAM	Age 23; unemployed but 'fiddle' work; GCSEs (low grades); NVQ levels 1 & 2; lives with child; some recreational drug use; shoplifting when young.	Age 27; unemployed; no further qualifications; lives with father of two children; no drug use; no crime.
'Adam'	STW	Age 21; New Deal; low GCSEs; doing NVQ levels 1 & 2; parents' home; recreational drug use; no crime.	Age 25; unemployed; no other qualifications; parents' home; recreational drug use; no crime but victim of assault.
'Roy'	STW	Age 20; unemployed; YT; low GCSEs; parents' home; recreational drug use (cannabis); no crime.	Age 23; unemployed; no further qualifications; parents' home; no drug use, but two criminal convictions for drunk and disorderly.
'Chrissie'	STW	Age 21; unemployed; New Deal; low GCSEs; YT but no qualifications; lives alone; no drug use; no crime.	Age 25; unemployed; no further education or training; lives alone; no drug use; no crime.
'Annie'	STW	Age 24; no GCSEs; NVQ levels 2 & 3; Access course to university; F/T student; living with partner; recreational drug use; no crime.	Age 27; unemployed; degree (2:2); about to move into new home with partner; expecting first child; no drug use; no crime.
'Simon'	STW	Age 19; unemployed; low GCSEs; City & Guilds; parents' home; no drug use; no crime.	Age 23; F/T employed; no further qualifications; parents' home; no drug use; no crime.
'Marje'	STW	Age 23; F/T employed (hairdressing apprenticeship); low GCSEs; lives with partner; no drug use; no crime.	Age 26; F/T employed; P/T degree course; lives with partner and child; no drug use; no crime.
'Catherine'	STW	Age 19; New Deal; no GCSEs taken; NVQ level 2; lives alone; no drug use; no criminal activity.	Age 22; F/T employed; no further qualifications, education or training; lives alone; no drug use; no crime.
'Martin'	STW	Age 20; F/T employed; low GCSEs; lives with partner; no drugs; no crime.	Age 23; F/T employed; moved with partner; no drug use; no crime.
'Elizabeth'	STW	Age 19; F/T employed; low GCSEs; parents' home; no drugs; no crime.	Age 23; F/T employed; no further qualifications, education or training; lives with parents; no drug use; no crime.
'Alex'	STW	Age 23; New Deal; low GCSEs; YT but no NVQ; lives with parents; no drug use; no crime.	Age 25; F/T employed; doing NVQ level 2; lives with parents; no drug use; no crime.
'Carol-Anne'	STW	Age 24; F/T employed; GCSE passes; NVQ levels 1, 2 & 3; moved to live with partner; no drug use; no crime.	Age 28; unemployed; no further qualifications, education or training; lives with partner; one child; no drug use; no crime.